CONTENTS

ACKNOWLEDGEMENTS

My grateful thanks go to the following people:

Dawn Gunby, who did all the excellent drawings – although she still hasn't taken up judo!

Members of Kendal Judo Club, who once again endured being posed, poked, pulled and generally manoeuvred into the positions I wanted for Dawn's drawings. That they did this with enthusiasm and without complaint is due to the club's commitment to the sport of judo.

Bob Willingham, whose expertise behind a camera is obvious when you look at the photographs which accompany this book.

Dr Ken Kingsbury, Rossalyn Elliott, Hilary Hector, Jean McNaughton and **Nicholas Soames** for their expert opinions and help.

All my many friends and **fellow** *judoka* whose encouragement helped this book come to fruition.

Finally, to **Tony Macconnell** for his expert help and his encouragement throughout the 30 years I have been in judo. His dedication to the sport, not just for players at the top but also with the beginners in the sport, epitomizes the expression 'The spirit of Judo'. This book is dedicated to him.

Domo arigato gozaimasu

(Note: All references to male players may be taken to include females and vice versa.)

CONVERSION TABLE

1 millimetre (mm)	= 0.03 inch
1 centimetre (cm)	= 0.93 inch
1 metre (m)	= 1.09 yards, 3.28 feet
1 kilometre (km)	= 0.62 mile
1 gram (g)	= 0.03 ounce
1 kilogram (kg)	= 2.20 pounds, 0.15 stone
1 millilitre (ml)	= 0.03 fluid ounce

Temperature conversion

$$°C = (°F - 32) \times 5$$

GET TO GRIPS WITH

COMPETITION JUDO

Peter Holme

WARD LOCK

A WARD LOCK BOOK

First published 1996 by Ward Lock
A Cassell Imprint
Cassell plc, Wellington House
125 Strand
London WC2R 0BB

Distributed in the United States by
Sterling Publishing Co., Inc.
387 Park Avenue South, New York, NY 10016–8810

Distributed in Australia by
Capricorn Link (Australia) Pty Ltd
2/13 Carrington Road, Castle Hill, NSW 2154

British Library Cataloguing-in-Publication Data
A catalogue entry for this title is available from
the British Library

ISBN 0-7063-7539-4

Design and computer make-up by
Tony & Penny Mills
Wrentham, Suffolk

Printed and bound in Great Britain
by the Bath Press, Bath

Front cover: Rendle vs Merah. Photograph by Bob
Willingham.

PREFACE

Judo is a sport that started in Japan but now has players in virtually every country of the world. This book is for people who have some experience of the sport and who have, by now, improved to green, blue or low brown belts. It is aimed at two sorts of *judoka*: those of you who prefer to progress past the grading stage and into competitions and those who perhaps feel that competitions are not for them but want to continue with the pastime. The following pages cover the interests of both.

For the competitor there is diet, weight training and stretching exercises as well as descriptions of championship winning techniques and the dangers of drugs. For the non-fighter there are chapters on becoming a referee and how competitions are run. Being an official can be just as interesting and challenging, and you usually get to watch the best judo for free. There is also information for budding coaches who wish to help their players win tournaments.

You never stop learning with judo, and I hope that this book will give you the opportunity to get a firmer grip on the Olympic sport of judo.

Here are the encouraging words of a sign that has hung on the walls of Kendal Judo Club's *dojo* for many years:

Better to dare mighty things
Than be among those timid souls
Who know neither victory or defeat

Peter Holme

1 A BRIEF HISTORY OF COMPETITION JUDO

Dr Jigoro Kano, who first formulated judo in Japan, never really intended it to become a competitive sport. Although he had adapted it from Japanese forms of self-defence, such as ju-jitsu, he saw it more as a discipline and certainly not as a sport. There it might have stayed but for the fact that Jigoro Kano was able to influence the Japanese Ministry of Education. This body was looking for some way of improving the physical fitness of schoolchildren. Kano suggested judo, not just from the point of view of bodily health but also because it was seen as producing spiritual and mental fitness. From that point, judo spread rapidly but, by the very nature of its techniques, it also became a competitive sport.

Judo was brought to Britain as a music hall act in 1899 by Yukio Tani, who challenged all comers on stage. Eventually, in 1918, he joined forces with Gunji Koizumi (who became known as the 'Father of British Judo'), and they formed the first judo club in Britain, called the Budokwai. By 1929 there was sufficient interest and activity to hold the first international judo match. The Budokwai sent a team to Frankfurt and beat the German team quite convincingly. Indeed, it was not until 1932 that a British team was defeated by the Germans in these regular exchanges.

The rules were then very basic. A player had to wear a jacket, stockings (we would now call them tights) and soft-soled shoes. Each competitor was entitled to the assistance of a second and three helpers. Each contest lasted for three rounds of three minutes each. Leglocks and spine-locks were allowed. There were no weight categories and the contests were decided on a best of three points.

BRITISH NATIONAL CHAMPIONSHIPS

It is interesting to note that European and World Championships had been successfully held before Britain started running a British Open tournament. There had been, in the run-up to the 1964 Olympics, National Trials held in London. However, it was not until 1965 that the first British Open Championships for Men were held at Crystal Palace sports centre in London. Seventy-seven competitors took part, only nine of whom came from abroad. One of the best contests was in the semi-finals of the middleweight category when nineteen-year-old Brian Jacks met George Kerr from Edinburgh (he was to become the Chairman of the British Judo Association and a Vice-president of the European Judo Union). The Scot won by a unanimous decision at the end of the contest and went on to win the title. Only two other British players won gold medals: George Glass and Ray Ross.

Women's competitive judo was officially recognized the following year (1966) with the advent of the Women's Team Championships. They were held in Liverpool – and behind closed doors. In addition to the normal scores there were judges who gave marks on style and movement, which were also used in the decision as to who had won a contest. In 1969 the event moved to Crystal Palace, although still behind drawn curtains so that 'casual visitors to the Centre could not observe the women fighting' (contemporary report).

It was not until 1971 that the first British Open for Women was held, again at Crystal Palace. There were 109 entries, including German and Dutch players. BBC Television also attended the event – a very different situation from a couple of years previously. A contemporary report by John Goodbody claimed that the final between Ellen Cobb and the Budokwai's Jane Peach was 'more exciting than any in five years of Men's Open Championships'. 'Peaches' won the contest in which Ellen knocked herself out with a *makikomi* (winding throw), attempted right at the end. As a consolation, Ellen went on to win the Open weight category. Another British gold medallist was Chris Child, who was a stunt artist and stand-in for Emma Peel in *The Avengers* TV series.

Eventually both the men's and women's events were combined. First, there was a full weekend of judo at Crystal Palace and then, since 1992, the events have been held at the National Indoor Arena in Birmingham. In 1995 over 500 competitors fought in what is probably the biggest senior one-day judo event in the world.

MEN'S INTERNATIONAL COMPETITION JUDO

The first official European Championships took place in 1951 in Paris. It had no weights but the competitors were segregated according to grade – brown belt (note *not* 1st Kyu), 1st Dan, 2nd Dan and 3rd Dan. There was also an Open category. There were only a winner and a runner-up declared. The UK was represented on the rostrum by Chaplain and Gleeson, both of whom won silver medals. Geoff Gleeson also won the silver in the Open category.

These categories continued until 1957 when the brown belts were omitted and 4th Dans included. The European Judo Union (EJU) also included three weight groups (under 68kg, under 80kg, over 80kg), plus an Open weight. In 1962 the players were split even further with the weights being divided into 'amateur' and 'instructor' classes. There were also two Open weights. At Geneva, in 1963, the grade categories were eliminated but the weights were still divided into 'amateurs' and 'instructors'.

In 1965 the weights increased to under 63kg, under 70kg, under 80kg, under 93kg, over 93kg and Open, but the amateurs were still not allowed to mix with the instructors. It was not until the following year that this division was removed and everyone fought just in weight categories.

World Championships

The first World Championships for Men were held in 1956 in Japan; 21 countries took part. As in Europe, these competitions were not held in weight categories so gold and silver medallists

Neil Adams (facing camera), the UK's first and only male World judo champion.

were the heavier Japanese competitors. Anton Geesink from Holland took third place. The second tournament also took place in Tokyo but the third World event was staged in Paris in 1961. It was still an Open weight category; here Geesink beat Sone of Japan for the gold medal.

The first British World medal was won by Brian Jacks. Fighting at under 80 kg, Brian won a bronze medal at Salt Lake City, Utah, in 1967. British Judo has only ever held one men's World title when Neil Adams (see the photograph above) beat the All-Japan champion Jiro Kase with *juji-*

gatame (straight armlock) in the under 78 kg category at Maastricht in 1981.

WOMEN'S INTERNATIONAL COMPETITION JUDO

Judo in the early years was, in the main, a chauvinistic sport, and women were discouraged from competing. A typical example involved an American woman, Rusty Kanakogi, who won the New York Championships, disguised as a man, in the mid 1950s. When it was revealed that 'he' was, in fact, a 'she' the medal was taken from her! The words 'for Men' were then inserted into the Championship title to make sure the organizers could not be embarrassed again.

The EJU has always encouraged women's judo and it instituted a Championships for Women in 1974. The first one was held as an experiment and proved such a success that the first official Women's European Championships were held the following year in Munich. Chris Child, fighting in the over 72 kg weight group, was the only British player to win a gold medal. However, Kathy Nichol (under 61 kg), Geraldine Harmon (under 72 kg), Ellen Cobb (under 72 kg) and Margaret McKenna (over 72 kg) won bronze medals. This organization of top-class judo competition for women in the 1970s goes a long way to explaining the domination of European competitors in World and Olympic events in later years.

World Championships

It was not until November 1980, following immense pressure from people like Rusty, that a Women's World Championship was held, ironically in New York. The UK came away with its first World judo champion in the petite form of Jane Bridge from Lancashire. She weighed in at well under 48 kg! Added to Jane's gold was a silver medal for Dawn Netherwood and three bronze medals awarded to Bridget McCarthy, Loretta Doyle and Avril Malley. Jane was also presented with a trophy for the most stylish player of the Championships.

Karen Briggs from Hull, won the World Championships four times and Sharon Rendle, also from Humberside, had the distinction of holding the Yorkshire, British, European, Commonwealth, World and Olympic titles all at the same time – a unique claim from any athlete in any sport in this country. Other women's World champions over the years include Diane Bell (see the photograph on p.42) and Ann Hughes. In the 1993 World Championships Nicola Fairbrother kept Britain's tradition of at least one World champion every time the competition has been held (with the exception of 1991).

THE OLYMPIC GAMES

Jigoro Kano, a life-long supporter of the Olympic ideals, died on board a liner on his way to a meeting which was almost certain to accept Japan's offer to host the 1940 Olympic Games. Had the Second World War not intervened it is highly likely that judo would have been accepted into the Olympic fold at that time. However, it was not until the Tokyo Olympic Games in 1964 that judo was included.

There was a great deal of discussion before its inclusion. The International Olympic Committee (IOC) insisted that there should be weight categories. The

Tokyo Kodokan resisted this 'intrusion' for a long time but eventually capitulated when it was seen that the IOC was not going to back down.

Aftér much discussion the weights were decided as lightweight (under 68 kg), middleweight (under 80 kg), heavyweight (over 80 kg) and the traditional Open weight. The contests were of 10-minutes duration for the eliminations and 15 minutes for the final. No scores were shown, just the time of the contest.

It was expected to be a 'walk-over' for the Japanese competitors with the rest of the world picking up the minor medals. This was so in the first three categories but, in the Open weight, a giant Dutchman, Anton Geesink, was in the final against Akio Kaminaga of Japan. The contest lasted just over nine minutes. A poorly applied *uranage* (rear throw) by the Dutchman took both players to the ground and gave Geesink an opportunity to apply *kesagatame* (scarf hold). Thirty seconds later, to an almost silent hall, he became Olympic champion.

Politics kept judo out of the 1968 Games. However thanks to sterling efforts by the then International Judo Federation's (IJF) President, Charles Palmer, it was brought back into the Olympic Games, which were to be held in Munich in 1972. With judo, the UK started the most successful run of any British sport in the Olympics. (Counting medal to player ratio, judo is the most successful UK sport and has won medals in every Games since 1972.)

The number of weight categories had now increased to six (under 63 kg, under 70 kg, under 80 kg, under 93kg, over 93 kg and Open). Britain's Dave Starbrook fought Shota Chochosvili of the USSR in the final of the under-93-kg category. The strange form of knockout used at these Games meant that the two had already met in the early rounds when Dave had beaten Chochosvilli . Sadly, in the final he lost on a decision. The next British medallist was Brian Jacks. Brian had taken part in the first Games in Tokyo without success. In Munich he lost only to the eventual gold medallist, Shinobu Sekine of Japan, and was awarded the bronze medal.

In the Open weight, Angelo Parisi was probably the lightest competitor taking part in that category. He did well, losing only to Kuznetsov of the USSR and coming back to take a bronze medal. Parisi then took French citizenship and came back in the 1980 and 1984 Games to win two medals: gold (over 93 kg) and silver (Open) in Moscow . He also won a silver medal (over 95 kg) in Los Angeles four years later. To win Olympic medals for two countries is unique in judo, and rare in any sport.

At Montreal in 1976 Dave Starbrook won a bronze medal for the UK (under 93 kg), which was his second Olympic win. Keith Remfrey, who had gone out in the first round in Munich, did exactly the opposite this time – going through to the final only to be beaten by Haruki Uemura of Japan. Nevertheless, he won a well-deserved silver medal. Brian Jacks looked as if he would win another bronze medal until the judges removed a penalty awarded to his opponent at the end of the contest.

Japan boycotted the Moscow Olympics but there were medals for Arthur Mapp (bronze) in the Open weight with a superb *de ashi harai* (sweeping ankle throw) and a silver for Neil Adams, who lost to Ezio Gamba of Italy.

In Los Angeles (1984) Neil Adams was strongly tipped to become the UK's first Olympic judo gold medallist. He looked completely in control of his opponent, Frank Wieneke (West Germany), when a slight lapse of concentration allowed the German an entrance for *seoinage* (shoulder throw) and *ippon*. Even Weineke could not believe it at first! Adams won the silver, and there were also bronze medals for Neil Eckersley with his, by now famous, hold-down, and for Kerrith Brown. Kerrith beat Nakanishi (Japan), who had been the favourite for the gold medal.

In Seoul, Dennis Stewart's heroic fight for his bronze medal was completely overshadowed by the previous day's disqualification of Kerrith Brown for a positive drugs test. Nevertheless, it kept up the UK's tally of a medal in every Games.

Women's judo was also in the Olympic Games for the first time in Seoul in 1988. On this occasion it was only called a 'demonstration sport'. Basically, this meant that the winners could not call themselves Olympic champions. However, as the selections made by the IJF, the sport's governing body, were so hard it was unfair not to allow the gold medallist the full title. The players chosen were the medallists from the previous year's World Championships plus three of the top players from the continents not represented by any of the first four entrants. Finally, there was the number one player from the host country, Korea.

There were some unfortunate anomalies, such as the omission of four-times World champion, Karen Briggs. Karen was injured in the early rounds of the 1987 Championships in Essen and never made the rostrum; as a result, she did not qualify for the Olympic Games. Jessica Gal was the European representative (she had won a bronze at the 1987 World Championships) and the IJF could not be persuaded to include Karen in the line-up, despite the fact that she had convincingly beaten all the other entrants on previous occasions. Sharon Rendle (under 52 kg) and Diane Bell (under 61 kg) both won gold medals, showing the strength of women's judo in the UK.

At Barcelona in 1992 I feel that the poor refereeing probably left the UK without a gold medal. Nicola Fairbrother came closest and would have won if the referee had not called 'Matte' (translates literally as 'wait', which stops the contest and brings the players back to their feet in the centre of the contest area) in the middle of the strangle that was working. She had to be content with a silver medal. Ray Stevens was also very close to armlocking his opponent in the final of the under-95-kg category but he, also, had to settle for a silver medal. Josie Horton, Kate Howey and Sharon Rendle all won bronze medals and British judo won a fifth of the total number of medals won by UK competitors at the Games.

2 MOBILITY AND EXERCISE

WARM-UPS – ARE THEY NECESSARY?

A great number of injuries, particularly soft tissue injuries, occur because the player has not warmed up. You might retort thar you did some exercises before going on the mat one time and pulled a muscle! The question that must then be asked is: were they the right exercises?

The purpose of warm-up is to accustom all the tissues of the body – muscles, ligaments, tendons and joints – to the range and velocity of movements they will have to go through on the mat. This is important both before a training session and before a competition.

Think about warming-up systematically. Think about all the joints and the kind of movements you make and then go through a warming-up procedure that covers those requirements. Don't just do the kind of exercises you've been taught without thinking about them. It may be that you are particularly stiff or have difficulty in the movement of a certain part. You therefore have to warm up with one particular exercise rather than others.

CLUB WARM-UP PERIOD

There has recently been a trend for clubs to dispense with a warm-up period. This is a mistake. Even today you will notice the Japanese national squad will do up to two hours warm-up before they compete. They do not have to be the traditional exercises as long as it is not a full contest or judo session.

Every young (or not-so-young) player should set aside time for a warm-up and mobilization exercises. It will help them to get *ippons* instead of *kokas*. More importantly, it will keep them on the judo mat much longer instead of sitting at the edge with a frustrating injury.

COMPETITION WARM-UPS ARE EVEN MORE NECESSARY!

At a training session in a club the atmosphere is normally relaxed. The warm-up periods are usually organized and, providing you follow the advice in this chapter, serve their purpose in making your body ready for the activity which is to follow. One other advantage is that the club session is virtually continuous, i.e. arrive, warm-up, skill training, *randori*, warm-down, shower, go home.

At a competition the activity routine is very different. You arrive at the venue, probably fairly tense, weigh-in/book-in, then find out when your category is competing, which may be several hours away. It is fairly obvious that it is no good warming up at 9 a.m. if you are not fighting until 1 p.m.

Get changed about an hour before you are due to start fighting. Put on a warm track suit, especially during the winter, and do not forget a pair of warm socks for your feet. As your category is called to fight, go into your warm-up routine. This should have been worked out, and practised, a long time ago and should cover all the groups of joints and muscles – especially those awkward ones. You will not get long for this, but do not try a rigorous session without making sure you are physically warm (hence the warm track suit). Now you are ready to fight.

When your first contest is over, put on the track suit and socks immediately you leave the mat. Your activity during the contest should keep you warm for your next fight (unless it was over very quickly), but keep active. Sitting in a draughty corner of a sports hall will cool you down and stiffen your muscles very quickly.

In most competitions in this country there are usually the preliminary rounds, normally two or three contests, followed by a fairly long break, and then the knock-out round. If you are still in the competition at the end of this section there will be another long break to the final. Follow your warm-up routine before every session. Indeed, you should do this during any break longer than, say, an hour between contests.

MOBILIZATION

Warming-up and mobilization need to be considered together because it is not just a case of warming the tissues so that they are used to working at the speed, and through the range of movement and stretching. In mobilization exercises there is a need to think of *all* parts of your body from the neck down through the shoulders, the spine, the arms, the elbows, wrists (even fingers), the knee and ankle joints, and especially the hamstrings.

Different people require different sorts of exercise. For example, someone who sits in front of a VDU screen all day will require a different workout to a person in a warehouse who lifts heavy cartons, and he will be different to the company rep who drives a car most of the day. All three may be fit but they do not use the same muscles during their everyday life. They will therefore require to work harder on those muscle groups which do not see as much activity during the day.

Most of the traditional exercises seen in *dojos* throughout the world have been developed to strengthen those muscles we use most in *shiai* (contest) and *randori* (moving practice). By the time you get to green and blue belt standard you should be thinking of what is good for *you*.

You should, in fact, go through a greater range than you would expect to in a contest. In real-life competition you always tighten up a bit. It is then that you need a safety reserve of ability to stretch and move.

STRENGTHENING THROUGH STRETCHING

Movement is controlled by the muscles, which are attached to the various joints in the body by ligaments. Many books have been written on this subject but, put simply, the more supple the muscle, the greater the flexibility of the joint. The greater the flexibility, the more movement you can get out of the joint. This extra movement could mean the difference between extending the leg just that bit further to complete the *tai-otoshi* (body drop) or being able turn out of a potentially contest-winning hold.

Muscles work in pairs. One is relaxed (the antagonist) while the other is working (the agonist). So, when you push off with your leg, the hamstring is the agonist and the quadriceps (front thigh muscle) is the antagonist. As you pull the leg through for the next step of your sprint the roles of the muscles are reversed. The hamstring is relaxed and the quadriceps is doing the work. This obviously happens at a great speed. The more the antagonist can relax, the more it will stretch. This in turn allows the agonist to contract more and produce greater power. The last few sentences are a very simple explanation of what is a complex action, but I hope it explains the need for a systematic and personal approach to the subject of mobilization exercises and their application in training and before competitions.

Flexibility disappears with age. We have all wondered how a junior judo competitor can have the back of her shoulder blades and the front of her thighs touching the mat at the same time. When she gets older she will wonder, too! I specifically use the female gender here because girls and women are usually much more flexible than men. Older men therefore have to work much harder at these exercises than their young, female clubmates.

EXAMPLE EXERCISES

There are a number of good books * on the market to give you a full range of exercises. Below are described some muscle group exercises that can be useful for judo players.

Lower Leg

Stand about 60 cm from a wall. Place your lower arms flat against the wall and extend a leg backwards, keeping a straight line from ankle to neck and your feet flat on the floor. Keeping feet flat on the floor, push your upper body towards the wall. You should feel your calf muscles stretch. Breathe out as you do this and hold the stretch for five seconds. Repeat with both legs and then rest or move on to the next exercise.

As an alternative, position yourself as above but, instead of having your back foot flat on the floor, take your heel off the floor. This time, as you push your upper body towards the wall, try to lower the heel to the floor without losing that straight line. Repeat.

Upper Leg

Lie flat on your back with legs bent at the knees and feet flat on the floor. Raise one leg straight up in the air. Take hold of the ankle and gently pull the leg towards your chest. Breathe out as you do this, and hold the stretch for five seconds. Repeat with both legs.

To exercise the inside upper leg muscles (the adductors): Sit upright, legs bent and the feet touching sole to sole. Now press the knees towards the floor. It is easier if you use your elbows but there is nothing

---

* Including Michael J. Alter, *Sport Stretch* (Leisure Press, 1990) and Bob Smith, *Flexibility for Sport* (The Crowood Press).

to stop you using your hands. Whichever you use, apply the pressure evenly and breathe out as you perform the exercise. Hold the pressure for five seconds and release. Repeat.

Abdomen

Lie on your back, knees bent, feet flat on the floor and close to your buttocks. Your hands should be under your shoulders. Now arch your back until you can rest your forehead on the ground. Hold for five seconds and then relax. Repeat.

Lower Back

Sit cross-legged. Raise your hands above your head and, breathing out, lean slowly forwards until your hands touch the floor. Hold for five seconds. Repeat. (This is another good exercise for the inner upper thighs.)

Upper Back

Rest on your hands and knees. Keep your knees slightly apart and, breathing out as you do so, walk your hands forward until your chest touches the floor. Hold for five seconds at full extension. Repeat.

Neck

Sit upright on a chair. Put your hands behind your head and drop your shoulders. Breathe out and pull your head forward so that your chin touches your chest. Hold for five seconds. Repeat.

Shoulders

Stand, feet apart, slightly bent at the knees, arms stretched out in front, and fingers linked. Trying to pull your fingers apart and, with arms still straight, now raise them above your head and slightly behind you. Be careful not to bend the back. Hold for five seconds. Repeat.

How many times you repeat the exercises depends on how long you have been doing them. Do not overdo them when you start; ease yourself in gently. You should find them easier the more you try them. This means you should hold them longer and increase the repeats. These are just a few examples of exercises and, obviously, there are many more you can do that will be beneficial both for training and competitions.

It is also a sound idea to consult properly qualified physiotherapists. They can give you expert advice, even if only to tell you which workouts are suitable and which are not. You may in fact do many exercises but not the *right* kind and so may not be strengthening the specific muscle groups you need.

RECUPERATION FROM INJURIES

When recovering from injuries sustained either in training or competition self-control is the number one requirement. It is no good to return to the mat a week after you have pulled a muscle or torn a ligament. At best you will be unable to train properly and the session will therefore be a waste of time. The more likely consequence is that you will injure yourself again or make the original problem worse. This will, of course, take twice as long to heal.

In general you should not go back to judo until you have a relatively pain-free movement of the injured part of the body.

Once the injured area is better, you should ease your way slowly back into a full programme.

Remember that in any form of injury the muscles around the injured part waste a great deal. This is especially the case if it is a muscle you have injured or it is a broken limb in plaster. You therefore need to do the precise kind of exercise that will strengthen up that muscle to get it back to normal *before* going back on the mat. The impatient player will end up back on crutches or with an arm in a sling!

It may well be that you cannot get to a sports injury clinic for help. Ask the 'old hands' in your club. The many mobilization exercises seen in a great number of sports nowadays stemmed from judo exercises a long time ago. Most of these traditional exercises in judo have been developed to strengthen those muscles we use most in contest and *randori*. Many of the players in the early days of judo were very aware of the need to 'mobilize' to avoid muscular injury. This continues to be true today. Although players may not know the technical whys and wherefores of exercising they know it is necessary. They also know, because they were taught that way, the callisthenics which are most suitable.

However I cannot emphasize enough that you should not get too rigid when choosing exercises. The conventional workouts are always a good start for beginners. When you get to the green, blue and brown belt level you should be thinking of what is good for *you*. So everyone in your class, or training group, should not be religiously doing the same exercise.

Having got to the stage where you can move the affected part without discomfort then, and only then, go back to *randori*. You should start gently, and then begin to extend yourself at subsequent sessions. Be prepared to stop if the pain comes back. Finally, before your 'comeback competition', give yourself a hard workout. Be honest with yourself. Are you fit? Remember there is only one person who will suffer – you! If you decide you are not really fit, then go back to the beginning of this section and start all over again.

During a British Open, halfway through a contest, a competitor indicated to the referee that he wanted to tighten his bandages. This was before there was a time limit placed on such activities. The official gave his permission and the player immediately sat down and started on the wrappings around his ankles. Then he went on to those on his knees, followed by the elbow joints and, finally, his wrists. Much to the amusement and amazement of the spectators this took nearly five minutes. Finally all was secure. '*Hajime*' said the referee and Neil Adams, who had watched all this rearrangement of bandages with great patience, promptly took hold of his opponent and threw him with *uchi-mata*.

3 TRAINING

This book is not aimed at the Olympic medallist. For that sort of standard you *must* be training full-time, seven days a week, at least four training sessions a day. That is the *only* way to get to the top. However, all Olympic champions started, like you, as club-standard coloured belts. This chapter includes a training programme suitable for that standard. If nothing else, it will certainly improve your fitness. You may wish, after a few weeks, to improve on it. By all means use this as a basis for your personal programme.

GENERAL TRAINING PROGRAMME

Training isn't easy. For it to be effective it is no good turning up at the club when you feel like it. If you want to be 'competition fit' then at least three nights a week is needed. Not all of that time has, or should be, devoted to judo. Training will normally include circuit training, weight training and should include some stretching exercises.

A basic session should last at least two hours. This is the normal duration in leisure centres for any form of sporting activity. The period should be broken down into three sections.

Warm-up

The previous chapter gave a more comprehensive description of warm-ups and you should start these before the main session.

0 to 30 minutes

It is better to use this time as gentle *uchi-komi* (standing practice). Just walk about and turn into a throw slowly, lifting your partner off the floor only. There is no need to throw him. The same applies to *ne-waza* (ground techniques): turn your partner over, with only a little resistance from him. Then give your partner the same opportunity.

The tempo should get quicker as the half-hour progresses. Do not stay with the same partner – change to partners of differing weights and sizes.

The *uchi-komi* should not be static. *Uke* should be moving, usually in the direction requested by *tori* so he can attempt the technique in nearly normal conditions.

Another method of *uchi-komi* is for both players to agree on a throwing technique. As player 1 comes out from his attempt at a technique he takes a couple of paces in the appropriate direction for the throw. As he does so, player 2 moves in and attempts it. Player 2 now moves a couple of steps and player 1 comes in for the throw. And so on! This provides a constantly moving platform and also improves each player's speed, for this form of *uchi-komi* gets quicker and quicker as each player exits from his attempts at throwing.

30 to 60 minutes

At this point of the session a new skill should be introduced. Alternate between *tachi-waza* (standing techniques) and *ne-waza* (ground techniques). When learning throws, they should be taught and practised left- and right-handed (*hidari* and *migi*).

No more than one throw and one ground technique should be taught – more would be confusing. In half an hour there is no time, anyway, for more. Ideally, the throws and holds should be linked and not practised as totally separate techniques.

Again, *uchi-komi* can be used as a training aid. This time the whole class can, and should be, involved. They should be lined up at one end of the mat; all those who are *uke* walk (backwards or forwards, depending on the throw) with all those who are *tori* putting in the attacks over the full length of the mat. At the far end, those who are *tori* should complete the throw at speed. Now everyone walks back to the other end of the mat and the roles are reversed.

60 to 100 minutes

This time should be set aside for *randori* and contest practice, which are different from each other. *Randori* means 'free-moving practice'. The idea of *randori* is to move freely about the mat in no set pattern, attempting a technique when the positional opportunity presents itself. To perform *randori* properly there should be only token resistance from *uke* when *tori* attacks. *Uke* should neither fall over every time *tori* moves a bit nor should he resist with all his might every time *tori* comes in for an attack – hard resistance means it is contest practice.

The *randori* should come at the start of this period and you should then move on

to the contest work. If there is a competition coming up in two or three weeks those who have entered should be made to work the hardest. They should be put in the middle and have to stay there while fresh players oppose them every two minutes. As an alternative, three or four pairs of players are put in the centre of the mat. The players who score stay on the mat and fresh opponents replace those who have just been thrown, and so on.

It is during this part of the session that coaching comes into its own. The players are under pressure. The coach should be watching as they are fighting and, when the occasion demands, take a player to one side and give him advice on a technique he is trying. The player is sent back on to the mat with instructions to try just that technique for the next few minutes. The coach should observe, closely, whether the player is taking note of his advice. If the action is still not correct then the process should be repeated.

On one night in three concentrate this *randori* session on *ne-waza* only. Ensure that it is as hard as the standing sessions. During the *ne-waza* practices it is important that a player is taught and/or shown that he should not just look at an immediate objective. Too often, competitors are concentrating so hard on, say, a hold-down that they miss opportunities for armlocks or strangles, etc.

Although hard 'contest practice' should resemble the real thing, remember it is still only practice. Do try all those new ideas. If they don't work, you should not worry. Try them with another opponent. Get your coach to analyse what is going wrong but don't give up with the first failure. As we shall see in chapter 6, a germ of an idea can lead to an Olympic medal, but it does not necessarily fall into place easily or quickly.

100 to 115 minutes

The last 15 minutes should be used for a really rigorous fitness circuit on the mat. See below for ideas on training circuits.

115 minutes until the close of the session

Now is the time, as a gentle wind-down, to do those flexing exercises I introduced in the previous chapter. You are warm and you will find them more effective than if you do them totally cold. An additional benefit is that you will not be as stiff in the morning.

TRAINING CIRCUITS

There are many different training circuits. They can and should change depending on what part of your performance you, and/or your coach, are trying to improve. They can be as sophisticated or as simple as you care to make them. They will obviously also depend on what equipment you have on hand.

The circuit given below in the box is a simple one, given that it requires no gym equipment. It tests cardio-endurance, strength and recovery. It is also important that the testing is carefully scrutinized to make sure the criteria of the exercises are strictly adhered to. The exercises *must* be carried out in the order set down.

This circuit can also be used as a fitness test to measure a player's progress. As such it should be scrupulously timed every three weeks.

The tests are best done with players in

---

1. *Press-ups.* Feet together, hands under shoulders, chest to contact partner's fist.

2. *Squats.* Carry a partner of the same weight category as yourself on your shoulders. Your thighs should be parallel to the floor *only*, not a full bend.

3. *Sit-ups.* With knees bent to 90 degrees and hands on the sides of your head, raise the upper trunk (the base the of spine should stay on the ground). Elbows should be touching your knees.

4. *Burpees* From a full squat, with hands on the floor, thrust your legs straight back (feet together). Come back to the squat and then stand up.

5 *Shuttle-runs* Do this, if possible, over a 30-metre course. A base line (on the floor) must be touched by the hand at every turn.

TIMES

Under 50 kg categories	2 minutes for each exercise
Under 60 kg – under 65 kg – under 71 kg categories	2 minutes 30 seconds for each exercise
Under 78 kg – under 86 kg categories	2 minutes for each exercise
Under 95 kg – over 95 kg categories	1 minute 30 seconds for each exercise

pairs, one working and one resting. If possible, they should be supervised by a non-participant (a coach or spectator) to time each exercise and to ensure the exercises are done correctly.

The totals for the first four activities are added together to produce an overall score. Your results should be compared each time you run the tests. Test 5 can be measured by the number of course completions you make in the set time period. If your training is going well you should improve your score until a plateau is reached. This must be then maintained in your build-up to an event.

WEIGHT TRAINING

If you move on to a five-night training programme then you should reserve weight training for the non-judo nights. Weight training is much more specifically designed for the individual although you should start on a whole body programme. You should also find a weight-training coach to start you off. Bad technique in these exercises is more likely to injure than do you any good.

Weight Circuit 1

An example of a weight circuit, aimed at gaining strength without adding body weight, is given below. The exercises must be done in pyramid form. Each type of lift should be interspersed with exercises from the circuit-training programme. Weight training should *always* be done with a partner for safety reasons.

1. Cleans to chest (wide-arm grip) (Figure 1)

FIGURE 1 Cleans to chest (wide-arm grip).

2. Bench press (wide-arm grip) (Figure 2)
3. Bench pulls (shoulder-wide grip) (Figure 3)
4. Dead lifts (shoulder-wide grip)
5. Cheating dumb-bell curls (Figure 4)

Exercises 1 to 4 are done using a pyramid system. The repetitions are 8 – 6 – 4 – 2 – 1. The weights need to be just short of the maximum you can lift with each exercise. Obviously, this is not a programme to see how heavy a weight you can lift but one to increase your strength by repetition. As your strength increases, so should the size of the weights. Exercise 5 should be 3×20 movements at maximum weight.

Between each weight exercise a simple 'feet-up' activity, such as that shown in Figure 5, should be performed for a set number of times.

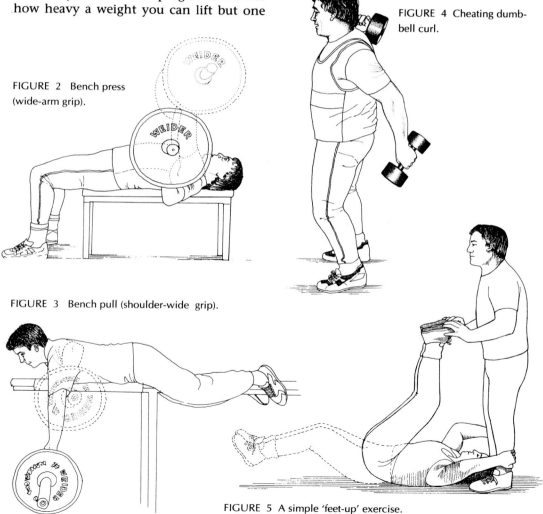

FIGURE 2 Bench press (wide-arm grip).

FIGURE 4 Cheating dumb-bell curl.

FIGURE 3 Bench pull (shoulder-wide grip).

FIGURE 5 A simple 'feet-up' exercise.

Weight Circuit 2

This one uses weights which are only half the maximum weight a player can normally lift. Each exercise is performed 10 times. The rest station should be the length of time your partner takes to complete one exercise. Each session should last six minutes (including the rest stations), followed by a six-minute rest.

For the first five days the circuit should be 3 × 6 minutes. The second five days should be 4 × 6 minutes. Then there should be 15 days at 4 × 6 minutes, but with an increased weight (50 per cent to 60 per cent of your maximum). If you find these exercises too easy, then increase the weight.

1. Standing press
2. Upright rowing
3. Press behind neck
4. Dumb-bell curls
5. Bench press
6. Rest station

There are a number of different types of lifts and these can be used when directed by a weight-training coach. For example, for a weight-gaining circuit it would be better to use:

1. Cleans to chest
2. Squats
   (thighs parallel to floor only)
3. Bent arm pull-overs
4. Dead lifts
5. Bench press

A typical pyramid would be:
5 × 100 kg
4 × 105 kg
3 × 110 kg
2 × 115 kg
1 × 120 kg
1 × your maximum weight
1 × failure weight

This programme is most effective performed three times a week. If possible, these should be on nights not designated for judo.

WEIGHT CONTROL

All the time, and especially leading up to a competition, a fighter should be aware of his weight. Remember that all the work training for an event can be lost if you have to put in a hard two-hour weight reduction regime before starting a competition.

Practising at a much heavier weight than your fighting category is self-defeating. *Randori* will be much slower because your techniques will be attempted in a different way. Indeed, the throws and holds used at your 'training weight' may not work at your 'fighting weight'. So get your club to buy a good set of scales, get them checked regularly and use them frequently to keep control of your own weight.

If you find it increasingly more difficult to keep your weight below a particular category then don't hesitate; go up to the next weight group. This is especially important for juniors whose natural weight increase should never be artificially restricted whether by diet or by any other means.

4 DIET AND DIETING

Whenever I was competing, even at gradings, I could never eat anything on the morning of the event. On the other hand, I have seen players, having just made the weight, disappear off and eat a full breakfast. They would then go on and beat all comers. Each *judoka* is different.

Full-blown competition means your muscles need more oxygen, which is carried around by the blood. This means that some of that oxygenated blood is diverted away from your stomach. Food is then slow to digest, making you feel uncomfortable and possibly nauseous. This tends to happen especially in a sport such as judo in which the body changes direction frequently. Liquified foods do not stay as long in the stomach and are easier to digest and, likewise, high-calorie foods are quickly absorbed into the system. Do not be afraid to experiment while training. Find the ideal meal and timing by trial and error. Once organized, stay with that format for both competition and heavy training.

Diet is not just used to lose or control your weight. It should also be seriously considered when deciding which food is best for what activity and what level of activity you are anticipating.

SPORTS DIET

A sports diet should spread through the main types of food:

Carbohydrate (sugars and starches)
Fat (e.g. butters, oil, pastry, fried foods)
Protein (e.g. meat, fish, eggs, milk, cheese)

The ideal ratio for a balanced sports diet should be 60 per cent carbohydrate, 25 per cent fat and 15 per cent protein. There is also one other factor to be considered in your diet at all times: fluid intake.

Carbohydrate

As this should be your largest intake it is therefore the most important. Carbohydrate gives you energy; everyone needs this just in order to live. The more active you are, the more carbohydrate your body needs.

However, if you do not use the energy produced by carbohydrate you tend to put on weight, so your diet has to be closely controlled. To do this you need an accurate set of scales and constant weight checks.

If you are serious about your diet then you should obtain the best set of weighing scales you can afford. Place them permanently on a hard, flat and level surface and check them for accuracy over your normal weight range. Small inaccuracies at the low end of the weights can, and do, balloon into major differences of 500 g or more at a heavier weight.

If you can, get some weights and check them. The alternative is to go to your local chemist who generally has a set of public scales. Check your weight on these, then go home immediately and see what your scales show. Bear in mind that the chemist's scales will be the ones which are correct as they are checked regularly. Either adjust your scales or always take into account the difference.

Your body only stores a little carbohydrate in muscles and the liver, where it is stored in a form of glucose known as glycogen. Glucose gives energy to the muscles. The lack of glycogen at the end of a hard contest or training session becomes obvious to a player: your arms feel leaden and you do not seem to be able to move as fast; you can't pull your opponent or hold him as strongly. This is known as glycogen starvation. Hard training improves your body's ability (and the muscles, in particular) to store more of this form of energy fuel.

There are two forms of carbohydrate. Firstly, there are sugars which provide complex forms of energy. They take a great deal of time to digest and get into the bloodstream, and from there to the muscles. Then there are starches, which are far more easily digested. They are therefore converted into energy much more quickly. Examples of starch carbohydrates are: bread, potatoes, pasta and rice.

Fat

Fat is not a major requirement for a judo tournament. It comes into its own in endurance events such as marathon running, where glycogen sources are depleted. As with carbohydrate, you should keep a close check on the fat content of your diet to avoid putting on too much weight. Everyone has fat, even if they look thin.

Protein

Protein is a very poor source of energy. Protein builds up the muscles which are then saturated by carbohydrate. Assuming a correct diet, the more muscle an athlete has, the greater his potential energy pool – but this only true up to a point. Too much muscle bulk slows you down and restricts movement, which is not good for a judo player.

'Complete protein', which contains all the essential amino acids a body needs, comes from meat (particularly white meat), fish, cheese, eggs and milk. I realize, of course, that this could be a problem for vegetarians. There is, however, another form of protein called 'incomplete protein'. This can be obtained from vegetable products such as grain, pulses, nuts, etc. 'Incomplete' means that they are lacking in some amino acids but, if you combine some of these vegetable protein sources (such as rice) with pulses, and wholewheat pasta with nuts, these will give you your required intake of *all* the amino acids.

Fluid

Everybody sweats, and therefore loses fluid. When you exercise you get hot. A 'thermostat' switches on when you get too hot and you start to lose heat by evaporation of sweat. Or, to put it another way, your skin begins to leak.

You must replace this fluid loss otherwise you do not perform as proficiently. You tire quickly and you get weaker. But you should be careful as excessive sweat requires a low carbohydrate content in your drink. With a low fluid loss, but a high work rate, you should pump up the carbohydrate content in the fluid that you drink.

Water is all you really need to replace lost fluid but sports drinks also contain essential minerals to help your recovery. There is not much point in using these during an average training session, as your normal diet will replace the lost minerals very quickly, but it is a good idea to add these to your diet on competition days. It should *never* be necessary to take salt tablets.

As you can see, fluid intake is an important part of your training as well as your diet. You should take plenty of fluid during training sessions. That way you get used to drinking when fighting, whether in practice or competition.

FUEL FOR YOUR MUSCLES

Nowadays, all sportsmen and women know they should follow a carbohydrate-loaded diet. This fills the muscle with glycogen. In turn you can train harder, longer and faster. The problem with carbohydrate is that you will gain weight if you eat too much. Exercise, of course, burns off the excess weight but it is nice to be able to strike a happy medium.

The best advice, when leading up to a tournament, is for you to eat what is termed a carbohydrate diet. But do you know what that actually looks like on a plate? The problem is that each athlete is different and will require a different intake. So a player of under 48 kg, for example, will have a much smaller consumption than someone weighing 120 kg.

I could give a long and complicated formula to discover the exact 'loading' you may require, but the easiest way is to reckon on eating about 8 g of carbohydrate per kg of body weight. Therefore the 47 kg player in normal training should be eating around 350 to 400 g and the 120 kg player

needs a massive 950 to 1000 g.

How do you find the carbohydrate value of what you are eating? You should be able to read it on the packaging in which your food comes. For example, three shredded wheat will give you around 48 g of carbohydrate (c-grams). A small tin of baked beans (205 g) has 28 c-grams. A large hamburger will give you 40 c-grams. A packet of instant packet soup will have a c-gram value of only 15.

CALORIE COUNTING

There is another way of working out which food to eat and how much – by counting calories. A 'calorie' is a unit of energy. The technical definition of a calorie is the amount of energy required to raise 1 g of water by 1° C. You probably performed an experiment in the physics class at school where you put some water in a thermos flask. After you had shaken the flask for a long time you then measured the temperature increase of the water. The amount of effort you put into the shaking can be described in calories. The usual measurement is kilocalories, abbreviated to 'kcals', which is the equivalent to 1000 calories.

Every sport has different energy needs, and every player in an individual sport also has differing needs. These are influenced, like the carbohydrate loadings, by age, weight, sex, your metabolic rate, how strenuous and frequent the exercise, etc. For example: a heavy judo training session is likely to use up to 10–20 kcal per minute, or it might be higher if you train very hard. A gentle jog will give you only about 7 or 8 kcal but hard shuttle sprinting will yield up to 100 kcal per minute. The energy you take out has to be put back in. As with carbohydrate, read the back of food packets for the kcal levels of each particular food. There are also numerous books on the subject which will help you select the right foods and the correct amounts.

WHEN TO EAT

It is better, particularly leading up to a competition, to take your food in frequent, regular, but small-quantity meals. One huge meal takes a long time to digest and the energy gained is therefore slow to arrive and may be too late.

Vary your meals so they do not get boring – boredom tends to lead to cheating and perhaps indulging in an extra chocolate bar. You do not have to be conventional with your mealtimes; if you fancy a bowl of cereal at 11 p.m., then go ahead. Nobody is looking! You should split your food into the four basic groups shown below.

There should be four servings a day from the first two types of foods with two servings of the other two types. Obviously, as already discussed, the size of the servings depend on your weight category, energy output, and whether you are male or female, etc.

FOUR BASIC FOOD GROUPS

Starchy foods and cereals	e.g. bread, potatoes, rice, cornflakes, pasta.
Fruit and vegetables	Take them how they come: fresh, raw, tinned, cooked, dried. Include juices as well.
Meat and vegetarian food	e.g. lean red meat, poultry, beans, lentils, eggs, nuts, peas.
Milk or milk products	e.g. Milk (skimmed or semi-skimmed), yoghurt, low-fat cottage cheese.

5 GRIPPING SKILLS

Kumi-kata (gripping technique) skills are both underrated and overrated as requirements of fighting *judoka*. They are underrated because, without a good grip, you are unlikely, in today's hard contests, to survive very long. They are overrated because gripping is frequently taught before throwing skills. This usually ends up in the situation of a player, having got hold of his opponent, not knowing what to do with him.

THE BASIC GRIP

This is the grip you will have been shown in your very first judo lesson. Grasp the opponent's left lapel around the height of his armpit with your right hand (see Figure 6). The left hand holds the outer part of your opponent's left sleeve at about the elbow. (If you are left-handed, unless I indicate otherwise, just reverse the instructions). It is a simple grip but one which is as versatile as any that you will come across. It allows you to throw on any side and from any angle. Although it is an all-purpose grip, it tends to leave you open to your opponent's attacks. With today's rules for wide sleeves and open jackets it is also too loose, and does not control your opponent's movements very well.

In the 1980s the competitive judo player made his suit as tight as he could

within the rules. It was not unusual for a competitor to have half-a-dozen jackets of differing measurements and he would keep changing these until the referee was satisfied. It was also not unusual for him to put on the original jacket before his next fight in the hopes that the new referee would not notice. Once you got a grip on this type of jacket you had full control. The problem was actually getting a grip, and this stifled attacking judo.

If you tighten the jacket, this time under your control and not the tailor's, then you will find your opponent moving more to your push and pull. This is a

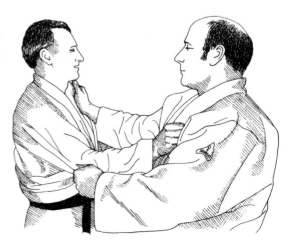

FIGURE 6 Grasp you opponent's left lapel, near the armpit, with your right hand. The left hand hold his left sleeve at the elbow.

27

much better reaction than when you appear to pull yards and yards of jacket before getting a reaction. The left hand grips slightly higher up the sleeve, about a couple of inches above the elbow. Take a good handful of jacket and turn the hand up and outwards. This tightens the sleeve and gives much better control of the limb and shoulder. The right hand stays where it is, but again take much more jacket in your hand. Do not close the thumb over the lapel. This restricts the movement of your wrist and prevents a sudden change of direction on your behalf. Now you have a much stronger grip and can control your opponent better.

CHANGE YOUR GRIP TO SUIT YOUR OPPONENT

Too often I see a 1.7 m judo player come on to the mat against a 1.8 m opponent and try to take a grip around the back of the head. All his partners at the club *randori* sessions are the same size as him and this grip is effective there, and it is all he knows. Remember that if you are uncomfortable the chances are the grip is going to be ineffective. Practise differing grips and if possible against differently sized and shaped opponents. Find the ones that are most effective and be prepared to change. Learn to adapt your throws from different grips.

Left-handed opponents

The average right-handed player fights *ai-yotsu* (same grips) most of the time. This is where the left-handed player has an advantage. Most of *his* opponents will be fighting with *kenka-yotsu* (opposing grips), which means that one competitor is left-

handed while the other is right-handed. When a right-handed player meets such an opponent he is quite frequently put off his stride when the collar-gripping hand comes across the same side as *his* lapel grip. You will also notice the left-handed player's hip is usually an effective block when the right-handed player attempts his normal throws.

It is now that you have to be prepared to change your grip. One effective method is the cross grip. If your opponent has a very defensive left arm, and is not allowing anything to pass it, move your right hand across to grip his right lapel (the side on which you would be normally gripping his sleeve). Keep your left sleeve just out of reach of his right hand. This is a good defensive position against a strong left-handed player. The left-handed player is now forced to step much more squarely in front of you in order to take a grip with his free hand. As he does so, take a high sleeve grip with your left hand, or even grip the collar alongside your right hand. You now have a strong hold, pinning him to the spot, from which you can attack forwards or backwards.

You must bear in mind that it is against the rules to hold the same side of the jacket with both hands for any length of time without attacking. This form of attack must therefore be quick *and* positive. Even if it is not effective your opponent could well relax that stiff left hand a little.

A taller opponent

I can remember, at one World Championships, seeing Sumio Endo, who was 1.9 m tall and weighed around 150 kg, pitched against Pak Yong Gil from Korea who, at 2.2 m, dwarfed everyone else. The contest lasted 13 seconds with the Japanese fighter taking hold of both lapels and throwing his opponent with *seoi-nage* (shoulder throw).

Endo had, in a previous contests, used *tsuri-goshi* (floating or drawing hip throw) just as effectively against smaller opponents. Here was a player who changed his throw and attacking grip to suit his opponent. The Japanese champion, for his *seoi-nage,* took a fairly high grip of the lapel and pulled his opponent down. Pak Yong Gil's immediate reaction was to pull back, thus allowing Endo to turn in for the throw.

The double lapel grip also allowed Endo to attack on either side without altering his hold, giving his opponent little chance of a defence as he did not know from where it was coming. A double-lapel grip is equally effective in a number of other throws such as *uchi-mata* (inner thigh), *seoi-otoshi* (shoulder drop), and *yama-arashi* ('mountain storm').

A smaller or same-sized opponent

This type of opponent is suitable for the grip around the back of the neck. A strong pull with the right hand brings the head down and forwards. The natural reaction is to pull against this. Release the pull momentarily and push your right forearm and elbow into the shoulder; this will start to turn him round to his right. A strong pull with the left hand speeds up this turn and centres his weight on to the right leg, which can now be attacked with *o-soto-gari* (major outer reaping throw) or *o-uchi-gari* (major inner reaping throw).

Care must be taken to ensure you have effective control over the head. Forward throws such as *harai-goshi* (sweeping hip) or *uchi-mata* are particularly vulnerable to a leg grab counter such as *te-guruma* (hand-wheel).

Figure 7, the last grip in this chapter, is the double-sleeve grip, and is not seen so often nowadays. Perhaps its demise was due to the tight-fitting jackets of the 1980s. With the new, loose-fitting jackets, it may well come back. As with the double-lapel grip, the attacks can be placed either side with no indication from *tori* until it is too late.

Sode-tsurikomi-goshi (sleeve-pulling hip throw) is the favoured technique (Figure 8).

FIGURE 7   The double-sleeve grip.

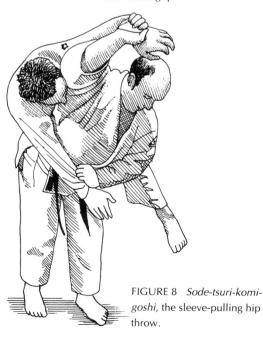

FIGURE 8   *Sode-tsuri-komi-goshi,* the sleeve-pulling hip throw.

Take a grip of your opponent's sleeve, knuckles facing inwards, about halfway up the forearm. As you turn into your opponent, the leading arm is pushed hard and straight up into the air, rather like a soccer player who has just scored a goal. The other arm is pulling down and round. If executed properly, your opponent will go straight over your shoulder and, with both arms trapped, there is very little he can do to avoid a high score.

EXERCISES FOR GRIPPING

Here is a simple exercise that can be done on your own or with a class. Hold both arms straight out in front, parallel with the floor. Clench and unclench the fists rapidly while keeping the arms outstretched. Start with 20 clenches and unclenches and then a rest, followed by another 20. The number of sets and the number of clenches and unclenches should increase. If you do this in a class, make a little competition of it. Who can carry on the longest? It is not a damaging exercise – your arms will give out long before your sinews.

Here is a second exercise that needs no equipment. Stand straight with your arms bent across your chest, fingers hooked together. Try to pull your hands apart as you straighten your arms out in front of you, parallel with the ground. Once your arms are straight out, pause briefly and start to bend them slowly into your chest again, still trying to pull your hands apart. Initially, repeat this five times, then rest and do another five. Again, increase the number of exercises and sets as you get stronger.

For another exercise you will need a piece of dowel, about 20 mm in diameter, with a length of string knotted through it and a weight at the other end. Stretch out your arms and twist the dowel, wrapping the string around it and bringing up the weight. Once the weight is at the top, reverse the twist and control the weight back down again.

This final exercise can be done at any time. Simply squeeze a fairly solid rubber ball. You should not forget to try this with *both* hands.

POSTSCRIPT

Finally, don't spend all your time trying to get your 'special' grip. Remember that the object of the game is to throw your opponent, not just to get hold of him. It will be of benefit in the long run to learn to throw from all sorts of grips and in all sorts of positions.

6 JUDO TECHNIQUES

One of the most penalized techniques on a judo mat is the 'drop knee' *seoi-nage*. This is not because it is illegal or dangerous. Frequently the attempt is so appallingly bad the referee considers it as negative judo and punishes accordingly.

It first surfaced as a serious technique back in the early 1970s. In the World Championships in Vienna it caught a large number of players, including Brian Jacks, who was thrown for *ippon*. It happens so fast that a poor coach misses the important reasons for its success. He just sees, and assumes, it is the dropping to the knees which makes it work.

However, performed properly, it is a world beater – as Nik Fairbrother showed in the 1993 World Championships. The four drawings of this technique (Figures 9a–9d) are from a series of photographs taken by Bob Willingham. He has kindly allowed them to be used as an example of the correct usage of the throw.

The most common mistake, when attempting the throw, is the entry. It is not sufficient to just drop to the knees. *Tori must* get between *uke's* legs (Figure 9a). To give him the space, *tori* should make *uke* move to his (*uke's*) left. As the left leg is moving outwards, without

FIGURE 9a Drop-knee *seoi-nage*: *tori* must get between *uke's* legs

FIGURE 9b *Tori* pulls *uke's* head down and forwards

FIGURE 9c *Tori* comes off his knees and drives upwards with his lower back

FIGURE 9d *Tori's* head and right shoulder also rotate while keeping a strong grip and close body contact.

weight, then is the time for *tori* to turn the full 180 degrees and drop to his knees. He should pull *uke*'s head down and forwards as he does so (Figure 9b).

It is possible for a quick-thinking *uke* to put his hand or arm down or even bring a leg round. This could block the throw and certainly help *uke* to regain his balance. At this point *tori* should come off his knees, driving upwards with his lower back (Figure 9c). The drive should continue, particularly off the left foot. *Tori's* head and right shoulder should also rotate (Figure 9d), while keeping a strong grip and close body contact.

All this should be done in a single smooth movement. A pause, at any point in the attack, will allow *uke* to regain control and the throw will fail.

The main reasons for failure

1. The attacker does not get far enough under his opponent. Frequently he is over a foot away from his opponent's legs, and there is no pulling action. The combination is commonly referred to as 'the flop and drop'. This usually allows *uke* to pull back and can lead to a strangle such as *hadaka-jime*. Often the referee calls '*Matte*' and penalizes *tori* for the poor attack.

2. If *tori* does get far enough under, he fails to follow it through by raising his backside and pushing his knees off the mat.

3. The movement of the throw stops,

usually after the initial drop. This allows a foot and/or a leg to come round and block the throw.

4. *Tori's* rotation stops. This slows the impetus of *uke's* loss of balance and gives the victim the chance to regain control.

MOROTE-GARI (TWO-HANDED REAPING THROW)

Morote-gari is generally thought to have entered judo around the early 1960s when the Soviet Sambo wrestlers (Sambo is a form of wrestling like judo) joined the judo circuit, but this is incorrect. The technique was, in fact, used from early times but was never really considered as a 'proper' throw. Gradually it has become accepted as part of a judo competitor's 'library' of techniques.

Although a very effective match-winning technique, like the drop-knee *seoi-nage*, this is also a much-maligned and often badly executed throw. Among the lower grades, and even among some high-graded fighters, this technique is usually used either:

1. As something to start a contest and make your opponent wary ('... but it won't really throw him').

2. A desperation attack when all else has failed and you are near the end of the contest ('... he might be caught for a koka').

Either thought is wrong. It is a very effective attacking technique in its own right as the Belgian Robert Van de Walle, Europe's most bemedalled fighter, and our own Kate Howey, can testify. It can fail,

like the *seoi-nage*, because the player does not understand what makes the technique effective. It is not necessary to charge across the mat, as most people seem to do, to attempt the throw. It can be more effective from a basic stance and grip.

Firstly, *tori* should get underneath *uke's* hands and arms as he comes towards him. He should push the hands and arms to either side as he reaches forward to take hold of the jacket. Another method is to sway backwards slightly just as *uke* attempts to take hold. This frequently makes *uke* overreach and puts him slightly off balance. Now step in!

Tori should now drop his hands to the back of his opponent's knees (Figure 10a). Lift upwards and backwards towards him

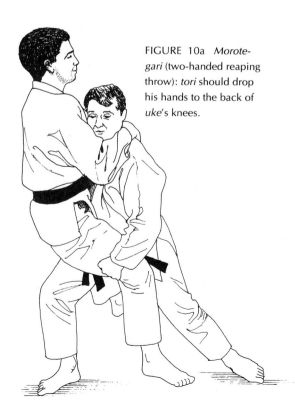

FIGURE 10a *Morote-gari* (two-handed reaping throw): *tori* should drop his hands to the back of *uke's* knees.

FIGURE 10b *Tori* turns his shoulder into *uke*'s chest; he lifts the lower half towards him as the top half is being pushed away.

in a reaping action. The attack should be with an upright stance and the lift does not have to be too high. The lift, as with any action of this nature, should use the legs. As the attacker comes in, the knees should be bent and the back straight.

This upright stance enables *tori* to turn his shoulder into *uke*'s chest. That contact should be kept as long as possible so, as *tori* is lifting the lower half towards him, the top half is being pushed away. The important thing to remember is that both movements go together and are continuous. There must also be a forward impetus as shown in Figure 10b.

The main reasons for failure

As with most techniques there are many reasons for failure; the main causes here are:

1. *Tori* charges across the mat, giving *uke* seconds to marshal his thoughts and create a defence. The charge is not necessary because it can be done from the standard grip and stance.

2. Too often *tori* comes in with his head down below the waist. This allows *uke* to stretch upwards. This may not effectively block the throw but it does give *uke* the opportunity to turn out of the technique as it progresses. This approach also leaves *tori* open to *sumi-gaeshi* (corner throw) or a similar counter-attack. Actually, if *uke* goes the other way and folds forward over *tori* it can be helpful, providing *uke* is not a great deal heavier than *tori*.

3. *Uke*'s legs are together as the lift proceeds. This can then block the lift against *tori*'s own legs. If this is the case, then the sweep by *tori*'s hands should be backwards and slightly outwards.

4. *Tori* stops the forward impetus once he has started lifting the legs. This allows *uke* to regain his balance; he is now in a strong position to stop the throw and possibly come in for a counter-attack. Either way, *tori* should get out quickly.

Sometimes *tori*, in the speed of the attack, misses out on grabbing both legs. All is not lost because, if he recovers quickly, it is possible to change into a form of *o-uchi-gari*.

O-UCHI-GARI (MAJOR INNER REAPING THROW).

As can be seen in Figure 11a, it is better if *tori* has a more upright stance for this technique. It does not have to come from

FIGURE 11a *O-uchi-gari* (major inner reaping throw): *tori* should stand more upright for this throw.

FIGURE 11b The leg should be moving upwards as well as backwards.

a failed *morote-gari*; it can be an attacking throw in its own right. What needs to be remembered is one of the 'Prohibited Acts' in the rule book which says:

> [It is forbidden] From a standing position, to take hold of the opponent's foot/feet, leg(s) or trouser leg(s) with the hand(s), unless *simultaneously* attempting a throwing technique. [my italics]

This is normally penalized by at least a *shido*.

It is therefore no good for *tori* to grab a leg and hang on until he decides what to do with it. Instant action is what the referee is looking for. As with all reaping throws, the attacking leg must be moving all the time the attack is in progress. Normally in *o-uchi-gari* the leg is sweeping outwards more than backwards. However, as you can see in Figure 11b, the leg should be moving more upwards as well as backwards. This can be seen more obviously in the photograph on p.36.

All the reasons for failure are the same as those for *morote gari*.

THE 'ECKERSLEY HOLD'

In 1984 Neil Eckersley won an Olympic bronze medal with a *ne-waza* (ground technique) move which was so original it

Patrick Reiter (Austria) throws Hidehiko Yoshida (Japan) with a hand-assisted *o-uchi-gari* in the World Championships.

was to take his name. Neil was first introduced to an original turnover by Nick Kokotaylo, the under-95-kg British Squad member, who had seen it performed during a visit to the USSR. Neil then adapted it and added several of his own ideas to produce the technique which came to be known as the 'Eckersley Hold'. It took him some time to get the authorities to accept the hold-down aspect. However, having gained the referees' recognition, the technique is now commonplace, like Olga Korbut's gymnastic back somersault on the beam. It can be seen at some stage during almost every judo competition.

The manoeuvre starts in a fairly common situation with *uke* on his arms and knees in a defensive position. *Tori*, astride his opponent, pushes his left leg through the gap between *uke*'s arms and knees. Then, taking a strong hold of the defender's left arm above the elbow, the attacker does a forward roll (Figure 12a). The roll should be over *tori*'s right shoulder. At the same time he should use his free hand to grab *uke*'s trousers and pull his opponent over on to his back (Figure 12b). *Uke* is usually in quite a weak position at this stage. Bear in mind he is also defending against a potential armlock (*ashi* or *hiza-gatame*) so this does not normally require an enormous effort.

FIGURE 12a The 'Eckersley' hold: *tori* does a forward roll.

FIGURE 12b *Tori* grabs *uke*'s trousers and pulls him over on to his back.

FIGURE 12c As he brings *uke* over, *tori* brings his right leg over and crosses his legs at the ankles.

FIGURE 12d *Tori* moving into *juji-gatame.*

As he turns *uke* over, *tori* also brings his right leg over and crosses his legs at the ankle – thus effectively trapping *uke*'s right arm (Figure 12c and also see the photograph on p. 38). Note how the attacker is holding his own collar to give him a strong grip on the defender's other arm.

The player on his back is now in a very difficult situation. If *uke* releases the grip that his left hand has on his own collar in order to attempt to escape from the potential hold-down, *tori* can move straight to the conventional *juji-gatame* as shown in Figure 12d. However, if he prefers to keep his grip, all *tori* needs to do is to swing his leg out and to the side,

Indrek Pertelson (Estonia) holding Shiniche Shinohara (Japan) in the 1994 Paris Tournament.

move his arm and body over *uke*'s trunk (Figure 12e) and the referee will call '*Osaekomi*' (holding). If *uke*'s struggles weaken that grip, with a quick spin *tori* can be back into *juji-gatame* in no time at all (Figure 12d).

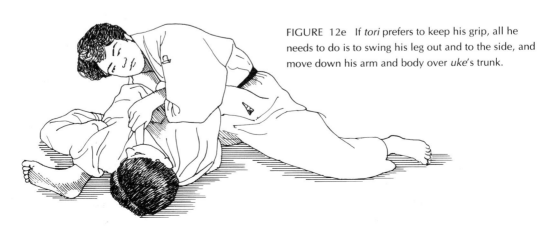

FIGURE 12e If *tori* prefers to keep his grip, all he needs to do is to swing his leg out and to the side, and move down his arm and body over *uke*'s trunk.

SHIME-WAZA (STRANGLE TECHNIQUES)

By their very nature, *shime-waza* have to be clean, sharp and quick. A slow, badly executed attempt at strangulation will, usually, leave the person attempting the technique wide open to counter-attack. *Uke* has got to be made to defend or attempt an escape from the strangle, and this defence has to be really strong.

So what have you got to do to execute a successful *shime-waza*? You need to apply strong pressure to the carotid artery or arteries which carry blood, and therefore oxygen, to the brain. The carotid arteries run up each side of the neck, and are protected by a muscle wall known as the sternocleidomastoid muscle. This is frequently referred to simply as the mastoid muscle. This 'protection' has got to be moved to one side to get at the 'soft' artery.

This is where the strong, ungiving jacket collar and hard wrists or fingers come into action. It will obviously take practice for you to get the wrist or fingers into exactly the right place but once there you will see and feel the effect immediately. Applied properly, a *shime-waza* could make a player unconscious in five seconds. It is therefore obvious that these techniques have to be practised with care, and preferably with an expert watching.

At one time it used to be considered very 'macho' to be strangled unconscious to 'experience the feel of sliding into oblivion'. It is now recognized, however, as a fairly serious injury, similar to concussion. Should a player become unconscious for whatever reason the practice or contest should stop immediately. The *judoka* should not resume play certainly for the rest of the day and preferably for the rest of the week. Often the player does not realize that he has been unconscious, and will quite frequently deny 'going out'. The coach or official must be firm and stop any further activity for that player.

Interestingly, women, in general, use very few strangles. Those that do find them very effective, as most women tend to submit earlier than men. Those women who practise *shime-waza* tend to be the ones who will persevere to the bitter end.

The *shime-waza* shown in Figures 13a, 13b and 13c comes as a result of a very strong defence to a *juji-gatame* attempt. It is a follow-up to the 'Eckersley Hold' mentioned above (Figures 12c and 12e). *Uke* may have a strong resistance by being able to grasp his own jacket sleeve. Perhaps *tori* does not feel confident enough to turn into the hold.

First, *tori* should try taking his arm (the one nearest his opponent's feet) through *uke*'s bent arm, and hold on tightly to his own collar and lean back (Figure 13a). If *uke* has a strong grip it is unlikely that this will be effective enough to allow *tori* to

FIGURE 13a *Shime-waza* (strangle techniques): *tori* takes his arm through *uke*'s bent arm, holds on tightly to his own collar, and leans back.

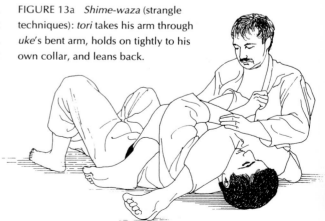

apply *juji-gatame* for a submission (Figure 12d). However, it has put the player underneath on the defensive. He cannot let go of his grasp so his arms are effectively trapped. Now *tori* takes the hand that is nearest *uke*'s head and gets a strong hold of *uke*'s collar (Figure 13b). If he now leans a little further back the *shime-waza* should be possible.

If *uke* does nothing he is likely to submit to the strangle. If he attempts to remove the attacking hand or leg, he has

to release his own grip of his sleeve and *tori* should immediately move into *juji-gatame*. Remember, for the best effect, to keep that thumb uppermost.

Here are some additional pointers to make the strangle more effective:

1. You should try to make sure that either the wristbone or fingers are across the mastoid muscle.

2. Your hand, as shown in the Figure 13c, can also go outside *uke*'s leg instead of inside.

3. For added pressure you should cross your legs at the ankles, especially if you have the hold 'inside' rather than 'outside'.

OKURI-ERI-JIME (SLIDING COLLAR STRANGLE)

This is a more conventional and classic strangle, and one which appears in the

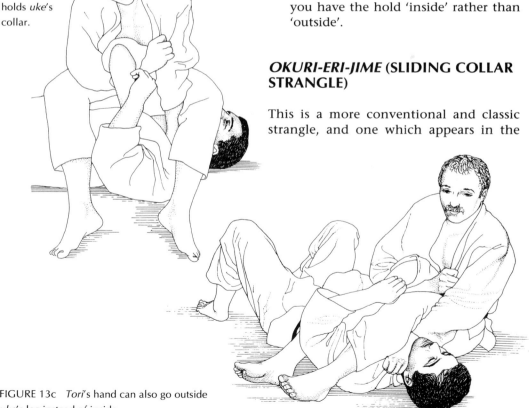

FIGURE 13b
Tori takes the hand nearest *uke*'s head and holds *uke*'s collar.

FIGURE 13c   *Tori*'s hand can also go outside *uke*'s leg instead of inside.

gokyo. The *gokyo* was the original syllabus of the Kodokan, which was the *dojo* founded by Jigoro Kano; this became the headquarters of world judo. Anything that emanated from the Kodokan was considered as unchallengeable well into this century. Therefore the *gokyo* was the base from which virtually every *judoka* was taught.

Okuri-eri-jime is usually applied from behind; I have shown the standard application in Figure 14a. The collar must be tight against the back of *uke*'s neck. To do this, the collar should be pulled tight with your left hand. At the same time your right hand should move across the throat and grasp the collar, with your thumb inside, as far round the neck as possible. To do this perfectly, your wrist joint should be pressing against the carotid artery.

Now transfer your left hand to the other collar and pull straight downwards towards *uke*'s waist. This should put pressure on both sides of his neck, on one side with the wrist and on the other with the collar. With *uke* on top and *tori* lying on his back, *tori* should be controlling *uke*'s legs with his own, as shown in the photograph on p.42.

1. It is important that the right hand pulls round and the left hand pulls straight down. Any other combination tends to take the pressure off the side of *uke*'s neck.

2. If you cannot get your wrist completely round *uke*'s neck for some reason, then the knuckles of your thumb should be used to press into the side of his neck.

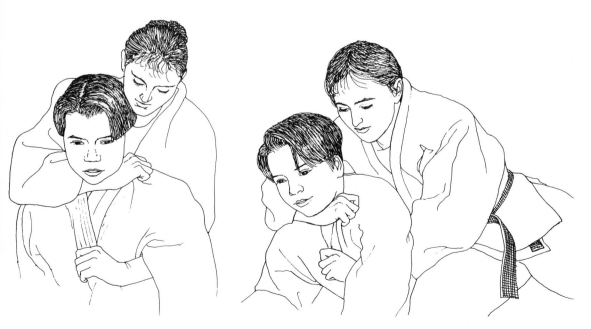

FIGURE 14a *Oku-eri-jime* (sliding collar strangle).   FIGURE 14b *Tori* attacking from the side.

Diane Bell (UK) strangles Qin (China) with *okuri-eri-jime* in the 1995 Paris Tournament.

3. If *uke* has his arms free, pulling at your arms or hands is more likely to increase the pressure. *Uke* should concentrate on pulling the collars apart. However, there is not much time if *okuri-eri-jime* has been applied correctly.

4. The conventional defence is to cross the hands and hold the lapels.

A variation of this attack is shown in Figure 14b. Here *tori* has attacked from the side. The positioning of the hands are as in in Figure 14a. In order to apply greater pressure on the neck, bring the right leg through and sit down on the floor.

KATA-HA-JIME (SINGLE WING STRANGLE)

This is very similar to *okuri-eri-jime* but, instead of putting the left hand through to grasp the collar as in either Figure 14a or 14b, take it up and round the back of *uke*'s neck. This will bring *uke*'s left arm upwards which, in turn, will apply the strangle.

KOSHI-JIME (HIP STRANGLE)

This is also a similar technique to *okuri-eri-jime*. *Uke* is on his hands and knees, as shown in Figure 15. Because of a good

FIGURE 15 *Koshi-jime* (hip strangle): *uke* on his hands and knees

defence, *tori* is unable to use his hands to attempt *okuri-eri-jime*. However, while on his knees, he can get a strong grip round *uke*'s neck, once more using the hard bones in the hand to move the mastoid muscle. Having got the grip, *tori* should swing the right leg through and sit down on the floor. As in Figure 15, *tori* 's weight should be across *uke*'s back. If it is not, there is a possibility that *uke* could roll out of the strangle (to his right). That will leave *uke* open, if *tori* is quick enough, to be turned into *mune-gatame* (chest hold).

There are a large number of variations on these strangles. Having practised the conventional ones, a player should now attempt the less orthodox approaches, as he would do with the throws. Strangles, like all other techniques, should be learned both left and right, including changing from one to another in midstream.

7 REFEREEING

You are standing in the middle of the main arena at the National Indoor Arena in Birmingham, there are about 2000 pairs of eyes riveted on you. A *hantei* (decision) is awaited following an exciting and close final. Whichever hand you raise, someone is going to be disappointed and may blame the referee rather than himself or his opponent. The audience, who are very rarely unbiased, are going to either cheer or jeer. A referee has to be able to cope with such situations.

DO WE NEED REFEREES?

Everyone of us, whether sitting as a spectator at a match, in front of a television set, or watching a video recording, referees a match. Many people make a living out of it. With the benefit of countless slow-motion replays you can deliberate on whether the referee/umpire was right. What people frequently forget is that the referee was not in the same place as the cameras and had a split second, not two hours in a video cutting-room, to make up his mind.

American football introduced a system in which someone could watch a video of an incident in a match and could overrule the referee on the pitch. They withdrew the idea after just two seasons. It was unworkable, and wasted too much time. They also found that, on the odd occasions

where the referee did make a mistake, invariably it balanced out between the two sides.

Try this the next time you have a *randori* session. Get your partner and yourself to score the attacks. However honestly you try, there will always be an argument over a *koka* which you claim as a *yuko*, a *yuko* which 'was more like a *waza-ari*'. And that is just in a friendly practice. Think what it would be like if the championship of the world was at stake and had no referees or judges. How many replays would be needed before the two players agreed even the first score?

MISUNDERSTOOD SIGNALS

Among the reasons for some of the 'discussions' following 'controversial' decisions is the spectators' and competitors' misinterpretation of some referees' signals.

Most signals given by the referee are fairly straightforward and easily understood. They are shown in the rule book. But there are a couple which can seem confusing.

Was it in or out?

This involves the corner judge (see Figure 16). In the drawing he is indicating that a technique/attack was completed in the contest area and it should now be considered

The British Open Championships in full swing at the National Indoor Arena, Birmingham. There were 500 competitors on eight mats in one day.

FIGURE 16 The referee indicating that an attack or technique was completed in the contest area and should now be considered for a score.

for a score. The fact that he has signalled does not necessarily mean there *must* be a score. It depends on the result of the action. If he waves his arm from side to side it means one or both of the players went out of the area before the attack was completed and therefore should *not* be considered for scoring purposes.

Until a couple of years ago the moment one of the players went outside the red area '*Matte*' was called, the fight stopped and the fighters brought back to the middle of the mat. There may have been a penalty depending on whether the referee/judges thought there was a deliberate movement to go outside the contest area. This included *tori* putting a knee outside the red during an attack. It would be likely to receive a *chui* penalty. Nowadays, if *uke* goes out during an attack by *tori* , providing the movement is continuous and *tori* stays in the area, then the outcome will be scored by the referee.

Negative judo

This is the signal shown in Figure 17. The referee will push his arms straight out in front of him, hands clenched and parallel with the ground. He then pulls them down to an angle of about 45 degrees and turns his hands inwards. This signal is given for one of two actions by a competitor. Firstly, it is given for a drag-down, where a player pulls his opponent into *ne-waza* without using a skilful technique. The offender will receive at least a *chui*. The same signal will also be used when a player has not been pulled to the ground. This can puzzle a large number of players, coaches and

FIGURE 17 This signal indicates negative judo.

spectators. In fact, the action by the referee is indicating 'negative judo'. A player can bounce round the mat and, to the casual observer, look full of action but a closer scrutiny will often reveal that he is doing nothing; all the movement accomplishes is the prevention of any action. He could also be excessively defensive, in which case the referee is likely to give the same signal. Whatever the cause, it is worth at least a *shido* to the offender and a *koka* score to the other side.

The current rules are about 56 pages in length and cover everything you need to know. It is a fairly major task to memorize them for the refereeing exams. A copy can be obtained from the British Judo Association Head Office, 7a Rutland Street, Leicester LE1 1RB.

WHO CAN BECOME A REFEREE AND WHEN

Anyone who has a love for a sport can become a referee. He should have had a reasonable competitive career. (One of the requirements to become a National 'A'-class referee in the UK is that you hold a black belt.)

You can be a competitor and a referee. Indeed, you should start your referee training at an early stage of your career. Too many top competitors think of nothing other than contest and training. Then, when their competitive career is at an end, they have nothing to fall back on and slip away from the sport. It is difficult, once your competition career is over, to suddenly change sides, as it were, and become a referee if you have not put in that initial referee training. The rules are now so complex that you must give some time to learning them. Top competitors may claim they do not have that sort of time, but this is a mistake. A good knowledge of the rules must be an asset when you are fighting – that way you can fight *to* the rules rather than *within* the rules. An excellent way to learn the rules is to become a referee. Next to yourself, a referee has the biggest influence on any contest you fight, and learning to see a contest as a referee looks at it is immensely helpful.

THE REFEREEING STRUCTURE IN THE UK

Area Referee

Minimum grade of 3rd Kyu (top blue belt) and a minimum age of 17 years. He can referee at Area events (BJA 3-star events) and gradings.

National 'C' (BJA Referee)

Minimum grade of 2nd Kyu (bottom brown belt) and a minimum age of 19 years with two years of judo experience. He can referee at inter-Area events (3-star tournaments plus selected 4-star competitions).

National 'B' (Provisional National)

Minimum grade of 1st Kyu (top brown belt) and a minimum age of 21 years with five years of judo experience. He can referee at National 4-star tournaments (although not the finals), providing there is an 'A'-class referee on the mat at the same time.

National 'A' (National Referee)

Minimum grade of 2nd Dan or 1st Dan with five years of judo experience and a minimum age of 23 years upwards. He must also have held a Provisional National Referee Award for at least one year. He can referee at anything in this country up to 5-star championships, including finals.

Some BJA Areas also run a Junior Referees Scheme for the higher-coloured Mon grades.

Each level of award is accompanied by a stiff exam on the rules, which need to be known word for word. If you are successful at the written examination you are then assessed while refereeing contests. The assessment is on various aspects of refereeing, including your voice, positioning, decisive attitude and, most important, appreciation. The pass mark is set high. Having gained your award, you are constantly being assessed at tournaments to ensure that the high standard of a British referee is maintained.

You should not go certificate hunting. Trying to get as high as possible as quickly as possible will not make you a good referee. Experience at each level is far more important. You should referee as much as possible, bearing in mind your competitive progress as well.

REFEREEING ABROAD

You will need to get to the top in the UK, and to have stayed there. You can ask to be put forward for the IJF award which means that, assuming you gain a pass, you are qualified to referee in Europe. The top grade of referee is the Olympic referee who, as the title suggests, appears at the most prestigious events and, in particular, the World and Olympic Championships.

8 COMPETITIONS

PREPARING FOR A COMPETITION

A competition may have been advertised in your area newsletter or *Judo Bulletin* and you decide that you wish to enter. When you arrive at the venue you may wonder what happens next.

At some competitions the contest charts are pinned up. It is certainly worth a look just to make sure your name is there. If it is not check – politely – with the competition controller. There may be additional charts but you could have been accidently left off. It happens, although not often.

If the charts are not displayed then you have to listen for your weight category being called. There is usually a timetable but you should remember that if contests finish quickly you may be called a little earlier than planned. So do not wander too far away. If this sounds a little simplistic, I can remember a British international player turning up at a British Open Championships five minutes before his group was timetabled to start. Sadly for him, the previous group had finished quickly and his weight category had been going for half an hour. He was out of the competition without even stepping on to the mat.

When you have finished the first set of contests and you are not too sure whether you are through to the next round, do not be afraid to ask. You will find that most officials are only too happy to explain things to you, although you may have to wait while they finish the job they are currently doing. Having said that, *do* not go to control table every five minutes to find out when you are on next, especially if the person in charge has already given you an approximate time. He or she could be trying to control up to eight mats (see the photograph on p.45, which shows a typical British Open Championships in operation) and it can be irritating to answer the same question time after time when you are trying to write out the competition charts.

HOW TO ELIMINATE COMPETITORS

Do you ever wonder how the finalists eventually get to meet in a competition? Why did they never meet earlier in the tournament, and why is it those particular two people? This is, in fact, carefully calculated.

On pages 50–55 some charts from competitions are reproduced to show how the systems work. (All the contests shown here are imaginary and the results bear no relation to what might have happened if they had taken place.)

In British judo there are four main

methods of getting the medallists in the right order.

Knockout (see Figure 18)

This is the simplest form of elimination. The players are paired off; the winner of the first contest then fights the winner of the second contest, and so on down the line. You then start at the top of the list again and repeat the process until there is only one competitor left who has not lost a fight all day. He is the gold medallist. In Figure 18 it's me! The person I beat in my last fight is the silver medallist (N. Eckersley) and the two players *we* beat to get to the final are the bronze medallists (N. Fairbrother and D. Bell).

You might say that this is a little hard on the player who was beaten early in the tournament by one of the finalists. It was only the luck of the draw that prevented him winning a bronze medal. This is true, and so judo introduced the repêchage, of which there are two types.

Simple repêchage (see Figure 19)

All the players beaten by the finalists, on each side of the knockout, fight their own knockout to decide who wins the bronze medal. The first player beaten by the finalist fights the second defeated player. The winner of that contest gets to fight the third beaten player, and so on until a player is left who has only lost one contest and to one of the finalists. He then receives one of the bronze medals. The player in the opposite repêchage receives the other bronze medal.

In the event shown in Figure 18 this would be, on my side of the knockout, competitors who lost in fights D, J and M and, on Eckersley's side, the competitors who lost in contests G, L and N.

Compound repêchage (see Figure 20)

This is a little more complicated. In this method *all* the first-round losers go back to fight for the bronze medal (not just those beaten by the finalists.) All the first-round losers fight each other, as a normal knockout. The winners then fight the second-round losers, and so on until the bronze medallists are left.

To ensure that two players do not fight each other a second time (except possibly in the fight for the medal) a little twist is made in the repêchage at fights I, J, K and L.

The advantage of this method is that the competitor on the wrong end of a lucky throw gets a second chance for a medal and it does not matter whether the player who threw him gets through to the final. Every player also gets at least two fights.

EJU repêchage

In European championships they use a variation of this system. In the EJU double repêchage those players beaten by the semi-finalists are the ones who fight for bronze. So you could lose out if you are defeated in your first contest.

Pools (see Figure 21)

In this method groups of three, four or sometimes five players fight each other in a little league. Any larger numbers in a pool take too long. If you look at Figure 22, you will see that 4 competitors in a pool need 6 contests; 5 competitors need 10 contests; 6 competitors will need 15 contests and so on. Ten players in one pool would need 45 contests to decide the

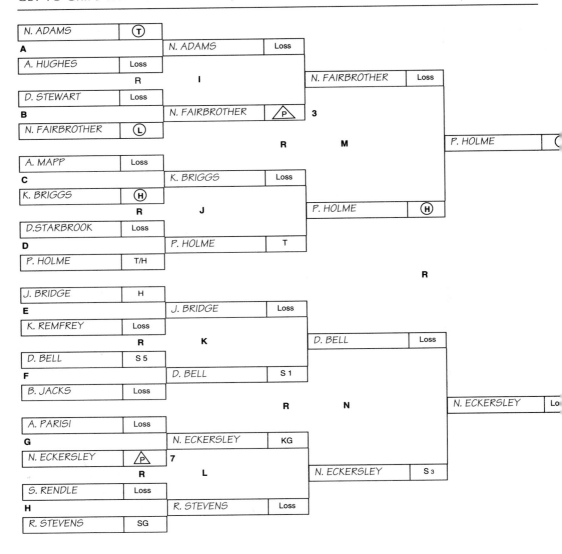

FIGURE 18   A knockout chart.

winner. Figure 22 also shows the order of contests. It is organized to give each player the maximum amount of rest between contests throughout the length of the pool.

In a pool, the winner is the one who either wins the most contests or gains the most points. This is the only time in judo that a *yuko* can legitimately be referred to as a 5-point score or a *koka* a 3-point score, etc.

As you can see from the example (Figure

Date	1.4.96
Event	WELLINGTON HOUSE TROPHY
Category	Open Weight
Round	1
Mat No.	7
Duration of contest	5 mins

RECORDERS/TIMEKEEPERS

Please print names – Do not use signatures

JEAN McNAUGHTON

KEN COULLING

MARSHALL TILLER

MALCOLM LIMRICK

REFEREES

Please print names – Do not use signatures

GRAHAM TURNER

RAY TOPPLE

MARION WOODARD

R= Result
Enter according to Normal Legends

Winner

P. HOLME

players with equal wins and points, those competitors fight again. The winning scores are timed and the player with the fastest time is declared the winner.

Usually the top two players go through to the next round. This can either be another pool or one of the forms of knock-out and repêchage already discussed. If it is a pool and the players meet again, the result of their first contest is carried forward. If the second round is a knockout, the only time they are likely to fight again is in the final which would take place.

The letters and numerals in the rectangular boxes are an indication of how the contest was won. The letter T in a circle, for example, indicates an *ippon* throw. A T without a circle is a *waza-ari* throw. The letter H indicates a hold; C is a choke or strangle; L is an armlock; S means a superiority win (a *yuko* – 5 points, a *koka* – 3 points, or a *hantei* – 1 point); and a triangle indicates a win because the opponent was penalized. The letters KG (*kiken-gachi*) show that the losing player withdrew because of an injury during the contest; SG (*sogo-gachi*) is where one player receives a *keikoku*

21), a player can actually lose a contest and still come out on top. Contest wins are counted first. If they are equal, the points are counted. If it is still equal, the result of the contest between the two players is used as the decider. If there are more than two penalty and his opponent then scores a *waza-ari* or vice versa. The letters FG (*fusen-gachi*) indicate that the losing player has failed to appear when his name was called; HG (*hansoku-gachi*) is a win due to disqualification of an opponent.

Legend | | **Points**

Ⓣ	Win by Ippon as a result of a throw	10
Ⓗ	Win by Ippon as a result of a hold (for 30 secs)	10
Ⓛ	Win by Ippon as a result of an armlock submission	10
Ⓒ	Win by Ippon as a result of a strangle submission	10
T	Win by Waza-ari throw	7
H	Win by Waza-ari hold (for 25–29 secs)	7
S	Win by superiority (yuko, koka or judges' decision)	5, 3, or 1
⚠P	Win as a result of penalty against opponent	
	(keikoku, chui or shido)	7, 5, or 3
SG	Compound Win (Sogo Gachi)	
	(Waza-ari score to player plus Keikoku penalty to opponent)	10
HG	Win by disqualification of opponent (Hansoku Gachi)	10
FG	Win by non-appearance of opponent (Fusen Gachi)	10
KG	Win by wthdrawal of opponent during contest (Kiken Gachi)	10
D	Drawn Contest (Hike Wake)	
	(Only occurs in Team Competitions)	Nil
L	Loss	Nil

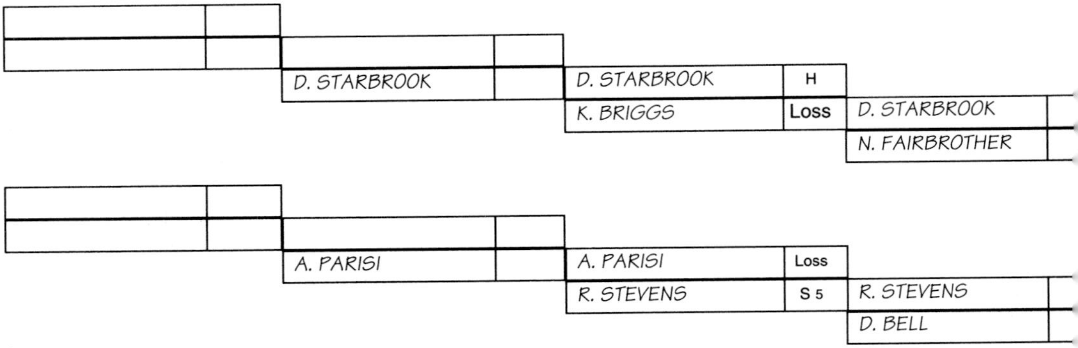

FIGURE 19 A simple repêchage chart.

In the UK, at specially named competitions, the points awarded for contest wins can be used to improve a player's grade. This occurs at competitions for 1st Kyu (top brown belt) and Dan grades (black belts). They can only score *waza-ari* (7-point) and *ippon* (10-point) wins. These wins must be against the same grade or better. They must also be as a result of a technique and not the awarding of a penalty to your opponent. In the knockout and repêchage tables reproduced

Date	1.4.96
Event	WELLINGTON HOUSE TROPHY
Category	Open Weight
Round	3 Repechage **Mat No.** 1
Duration of contest	5 mins

RECORDERS/TIMEKEEPERS   REFEREES

Please print names – Do not use signatures

RECORDERS/TIMEKEEPERS	REFEREES
HILARY HECTOR	GORDON MORTIMER
VICKY DAVIS	BILL HARGREAVES
DAWN BYRNE	BERNARD ORRICK
CHRISTINE DONALD	BRIAN MOORE

Bronze Medal

D. STARBROOK

Bronze Medal

D. BELL

on pages 50–54 I have omitted the grades to keep the contest charts as simple as possible, but I have included them in the pools. In Figure 21 you can see that only J. Birch has gained any 'promotion points' in his/her fight against M. Stonor.

HOW TO BECOME A TOURNAMENT OFFICIAL

The British Judo Association, which is the official governing body for the sport, has schemes to train tournament officials. This helps the sport in the UK and gives you another opportunity to watch and enjoy judo.

Like the referees, there are various grades of competition official.

Timekeeper/scorer

Although this may be the lowest grade of official in judo it is, nevertheless, an important job. If you are only slow by a second to react when a call of 'Osaekomi' or 'Toketa' is made it could be the difference between a competitor winning a championship or being a loser.

The timekeeper times both the length of the contest (stopping and re-starting the clocks on the call of 'Matte' and 'Hajime', 'Sonomama' and 'Yoshi') and the hold-downs ('Osaekomi' and 'Toketa'). The scorer alters the scoreboard as and when the scores and penalties are called.

Competition recorder

This official fills in the charts at the side of the mat and ensures that the correct players fight each other at the right time. He also ensures that the competitors wear the correct coloured belt.

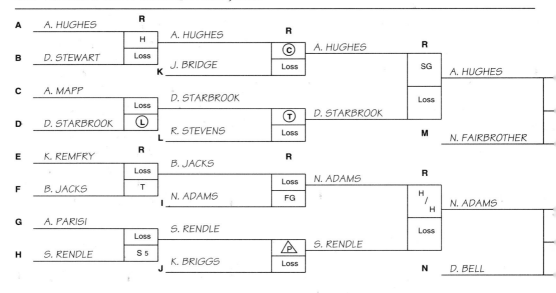

FIGURE 20   A compound repêchage chart.

Senior recorder

The senior recorder is usually in charge of a table at the side of the mat but he can also run small competitions. Senior recorders are expected to control a number of these events before they can apply to move up to the highest grade of competition official.

Competition controller

The highest award for competition officials. This grade is sparingly awarded. The person holding such a grade is expected to be able to run any type of tournament to any level, including international. The standard is extremely high. The candidates are observed over a

FAIRBROTHER
ronze

Date   1.4.96

Event   WELLINGTON HOUSE TROPHY

Category Open Weight

Round   3 Repechage   **Mat No.**3

Duration of contest   5   mins

ADAMS
ronze

R = Result   Enter according to normal legends

Letters **A** to **N** refer to contests on knockout sheet

It might also be worth while, if you are someone running a competition, to check that a player is not entered on the tables twice. In one British Open Championships a player had been entered by his country and also entered himself, but as living in a different country. He had a common name so it was not noticed until just before the quarter-finals when he was down to fight himself. He said, when asked why he had not queried it earlier, 'I thought I had fought more than the other competitors but they just kept calling my name to fight. At least I've had my money's worth!'. Sadly, he lost his next two fights and did not win a medal.

number of national standard competitions. Their ability to cope with all the problems associated with such an event is assessed. They then have a searching interview(s) before being given the award.

For further details, get in touch with the BJA, 7a Rutland Street, Leicester LE1 1RB.

Competitor	P. BLANDFORD		D. TAYLOR		J. BIRCH	
Grade	1ST KYU		2ND DAN		1ST DAN	
Area/Club	WATERLOO JC		MANSELL JUDO		MOWBRAY LC	
Pool of 3 4 5	Red	White	Red	White	Red	White
1						
1 1 2	Loss		10	ⓒ		
2 3					T	7
4	Loss					
2 3 5			Ⓛ	10		Loss
4 6	Loss					
7					Loss	
5 8			S 5	5		
3 6 9	Loss				3	⚠P
10			Loss			
Total Contest Points	NIL		25		10	
Total Contest Wins	NIL		THREE		TWO	
Place	5th		1st		3rd	
Grade Promotion Points	B/F	This Pool	B/F	This Pool	B/F	This Pool
					Nil	7
	Total to carry forward **Nil**		Total to carry forward **Nil**		Total to carry forward **Nil**	

Date	1.4.96
Event	CASSELL OPEN
Venue	WATERLOO
Category	OPEN WEIGHT
Round No.	1
Pool No.	1

Contest Duration: 5 Minutes

Please remember to insert points as well as normal legends for each contest.

FIGURE 21   A pool chart.

M. STONOR		L. DENSHAM		Duration	
1ST DAN		3RD DAN		of	
NEW ORCHARD		STUDIO VISTA		contest	
Red	White	Red	White	Mins	Secs
S 3	3		Loss	5	00
				0	35
	Loss			5	00
		7	H	5	00
				2	20
7	/P\			5	00
		7	T	5	00
	Loss			5	00
				5	00
		10	T/H	1	45
10		24			
TWO		THREE			
4th		2nd			
B/F	This Pool	B/F	This Pool		
Total to carry forward **Nil**		Total to carry forward **Nil**			

REFEREES

Please print names – Do not use signatures

L HARGREAVES

G. BAYLEY

E. TUNSTALL

RECORDERS/TIMEKEEPERS

J. SOMERVILLE

N. SOMERVILLE

P. HAUNCH

M. HAUNCH

4	5	6	7	8	9		10	
Player	Player	Player	Player	Player	Players		Players	
1 – 2	4 – 5	1 – 4	1 – 4	1 – 5	1 – 4	1 – 3	1 – 6	4 – 8
3 – 4	1 – 2	2 – 5	2 – 5	2 – 6	6 – 2	5 – 7	2 – 7	9 – 5
2 – 3	3 – 4	3 – 6	3 – 6	3 – 7	3 – 7	9 – 2	3 – 8	1 – 2
1 – 4	1 – 5	5 – 1	7 – 1	4 – 8	5 – 8	1 – 6	4 – 9	3 – 4
2 – 4	2 – 3	6 – 2	5 – 4	6 – 1	6 – 9	3 – 5	5 – 10	6 – 7
1 – 3	1 – 4	4 – 3	2 – 3	7 – 2	7 – 1	4 – 6	7 – 1	8 – 9
	3 – 5	1 – 6	6 – 7	8 – 3	8 – 2	7 – 8	8 – 2	5 – 1
	2 – 4	2 – 4	5 – 1	5 – 4	9 – 3	9 – 1	9 – 3	2 – 3
	1 – 3	3 – 5	4 – 3	1 – 7	4 – 7	2 – 3	10 – 4	6 – 10
	2 – 5	2 – 1	6 – 2	2 – 8	1 – 5	4 – 5	6 – 5	7 – 8
		4 – 5	5 – 7	3 – 5	2 – 4	6 – 7	1 – 8	4 – 5
		3 – 2	3 – 1	4 – 6	3 – 6	8 – 9	2 – 9	10 – 9
		6 – 4	4 – 6	8 – 1	4 – 8	2 – 1	3 – 10	3 – 1
		1 – 3	7 – 2	5 – 2	5 – 9	3 – 4	4 – 6	2 – 4
		5 – 6	3 – 5	6 – 3	8 – 1	5 – 6	5 – 7	6 – 8
			1 – 6	7 – 4	7 – 2		9 – 1	7 – 9
			2 – 4	1 – 2	8 – 3		10 – 2	5 – 2
			7 – 3	3 – 4	9 – 4		6 – 3	8 – 10
			6 – 5	5 – 6	2 – 5		7 – 4	1 – 4
			1 – 2	7 – 8	6 – 8		8 – 5	5 – 3
			4 – 7	3 – 1	7 – 9		10 – 1	9 – 6
				4 – 2			2 – 6	7 – 10
				7 – 5			3 – 7	
				6 – 8				
				1 – 4				
				2 – 3				
				8 – 5				
				6 – 7				

FIGURE 22   The order of contests in a pool system.

9 DRUGS IN SPORT

Throughout history humans have tried to improve their performance in many aspects of life by the use of artificial aids. These have ranged from sacrifices and prayers to the gods to the eating of various parts of an animal's anatomy. It is the same with drugs in sport except that, in the main, the use of artificial chemical aids can and does damage health. This makes the supposed athletic advantages gained – and it is open to doubt whether there is any improvement in sporting performance gained by the use of drugs – fade into total insignificance when compared to the pain and suffering which comes in later years.

SAY 'NO' TO DRUGS

Cheating by using drugs must never be allowed to become a normal activity in sport. Rules *must* be strictly enforced to protect the 'clean' athlete. Heavy penalties should be used to prevent pressures being applied to young sportsmen and women, thereby stopping them from abuse and dependence on substances which could, eventually, kill them.

The first lesson any player of any sport should be taught is to: **SAY 'NO' TO DRUGS!**

DEFINITION

The International Olympic Committee (IOC) Medical Commission have stated the following:

DOPING CONTRAVENES THE ETHICS OF BOTH SPORT AND MEDICAL SCIENCE. THE IOC MEDICAL COMMISSION BANS:

1. The administration of substances belonging to the selected classes of pharmacological agents: stimulants, narcotics, anabolic agents, diuretics, peptide hormones and analogues, and

2. The use of various doping methods: blood doping, pharmacological, chemical and physical manipulations.

BANNED DRUGS AND HARMFUL EFFECTS

Banned substances are grouped into various types, as follows:
1. Doping Classes
    (a) Stimulants
    (b) Narcotic analgesics
    (c) Anabolic agents
        (i) Androgenic anabolic steroids
        (ii) Beta$_2$agonists
    (d) Diuretics
    (e) Peptide and glycoprotein, hormones and analogues
2. Doping methods
    (a) Blood doping

    (b) Pharmacological, chemical and physical manipulation of blood
3.   Drugs subject to certain restrictions
    (a) Alcohol
    (b) Marijuana
    (c) Local anaesthetics
    (d) Corticosteroids
    (e) Beta blockers

1. DOPING CLASSES

(a) Stimulants. These speed up the heart rate but also constrict the blood vessels. Blood pressure therefore rises, which can cause serious damage to the heart. They induce anxiety, which in turn increases hostility. This can lead to loss of judgement. In judo this can be dangerous and lead to accidents. In a high-activity sport like judo, amphetamines have led to the death of athletes.

Stimulants are generally split into two groups. One group include the type of compounds that are found in cold cures and hay fever preparations. Amphetamine, pseudoephedrine, ephedrine, cocaine, caffeine, etc. can be bought in preparations sold, quite freely, in a chemist or supermarket without a prescription. It is obvious that if you buy such products you must be very careful. Check with the chemist, or your doctor, that it does not contain a banned substance.

A second group, which are known as beta$_2$agonists, are more unusual because they are also classed as anabolic agents (see below). They also include salbutamol and terbutaline, which asthma sufferers will recognize as being a compound used in their inhalers. However, when used as an inhalant, they are acceptably 'legal' providing none of the compounds mentioned in the previous paragraph is mixed with the salbutamol, etc. They cannot be taken by mouth or injection because they then become a very powerful stimulant and anabolic agent.

Again, you should always check with your doctor. Anyone who requires continuous medication of this or a similar nature, providing it does not contain a banned substance, should have a letter from their doctor giving details. The medical practitioner should also add a short note as to why it is required.

Caffeine, which is a banned stimulant appears in coffee, some colas, tea, cocoa and similar drinks, but the amount you would need to drink to test positive is excessive. To be on the safe side, use water or sport-specific drinks to slake your thirst.

(b) Narcotic analgesics. Strong painkillers, such as morphine, heroin, methadone and other similar products, are dangerous to sports people. Obviously they are well known as addictive drugs but their medical properties of subduing pain can cover serious injuries which will, quite often, lead to inadequate or improper treatment. The result can leave you a cripple.

Any form of severe pain is your body's way of saying there is something wrong. If the pain is so bad you have to resort to such drugs you ought to be in a doctor's surgery, *not* in a *dojo*.

(c) Anabolic agents. These are split into two groups:

Androgenic anabolic steroids. These include testosterone, nandrolone, stanozolol, methenolone, etc. They are the type of drug which everyone knows as 'steroids' when related to drug-taking in sport.

Testosterone is slightly different in that it appears naturally in the body. Excessive amounts can be detected and, if found, it will produce an instant ban on your sporting activities.

Beta₂agonists. I have already covered a couple of these under 'Stimulants'. Salbutamol and terbutaline, when given by mouth in tablet form or by an injection, have a powerful anabolic effect and as such are banned. Also included in this group are clenbutarol, fenoterol, salmeterol and other related substances.

(d) Diuretics. These include acetazolamide, bumetanide, frusemide, mannitol, mersalyl and spironolactone.

Medically, they are used for the elimination of excess body fluids and the management of high blood pressure. In sport they are used to reduce weight in a short space of time. They are also used to try to get rid of the traces of other illegal substances quickly by making you urinate a great deal.

The rapid reduction of body fluid can be dangerous. It can lead to kidney damage, heat stroke and nausea. The rapid loss of fluid does not help your stamina, which means you are likely to lose early on in the competition anyway. Like types (c) and (e) they cannot be bought without a prescription. Healthy men have no reason to use them. Some women are prescribed diuretics for fluid retention before menstruation. So, for female competitors, great care *must* be taken in their use before competition.

(e) Peptides and glycoprotein, hormones, and analogues. The use of, for example hCG, ACTH, hGH, etc., cannot be adequately explained in any healthy person. The misuse of growth hormones of any description can produce hypertension, diabetes mellitus and acromegaly (enlargement of the bones, particularly in the hands, feet and face). In certain circum-

stances it can produce Creutzfeldt-Jakob disease, which is a fatal brain condition.

Medically, those substances referred to in types (c) and (e), are used to induce growth and recover strength in people who have a genuine medical condition. There is no reason for any athlete to use them. You cannot go into a chemist's shop and buy them over the counter. So, if they are found in a tested athlete, he can look forward to a lot of serious questions being asked.

2. DOPING METHODS

(a) Blood doping. This is the removal of blood from an athlete while training. He trains while his body replaces the blood and then, just before he competes, the oxygen-enriched blood is put back with a supposed increase in stamina for the athlete.

The side effects that can occur are probably obvious: anaemia, kidney failure, jaundice, hepatitis, AIDS and metabolic shock.

(b) Pharmacological, chemical and physical manipulation. These artificially alter the integrity and validity of the urine samples used in doping controls. The intention is to try and make the sample look as though it does not contain a drug. As with blood doping, there is no medical reason for a fit sportsman or sportswoman to use this form of treatment.

3. DRUGS SUBJECT TO CERTAIN RESTRICTIONS

These groups are not necessarily banned products but they really give no advantage to any sportsmen or women, and judo players in particular. It is therefore pointless to take them and in some cases very dangerous.

(a) and (b) Alcohol and marijuana. These produce loss of judgement and coordination. A judo competitor is unlikely to last very long in a contest under their influence. Marijuana has recently been banned within British judo.

(c) and (d) Local anaesthetics and corticosteroids. These have to be medically justified to the authorities before they can be used. The justification has to be from a qualified medical practitioner and must be very specific as to how they are to be administered. They can only be dispensed under the control of a doctor.

(e) Beta blockers. These are used to control the heart rate in cases of heart disease. They modify the heart rate and are *dangerous* in a highly physical activity sport such as judo.

TESTING

The procedure of drug testing at competitions is simple. The choice of who is tested is made at random. If selected, you simply go to the drug-testing area (with a parent or other adult if you are under 16 years of age) and pass a sample of urine into a numbered bottle. Part of this sample is put into a duplicate bottle. Both bottles are checked and sealed in your presence and then sent for testing.

The test is made on one bottle (marked 'A'). If a banned substance is found, the second bottle is tested (marked 'B'). It can be tested in your presence if you wish. There is then the opportunity to discuss the issue with the governing body of your

sport before decisions are taken. If you are under 16, your parents or guardians will also be involved in these talks.

For your own sake, and that of the sport of judo, ensure you do *not* take banned drugs while competing or training for competitions.

Ignorance is no defence

If you produce a positive result, claiming that you did not know what was in the medication will not help in any way. It is your responsibility to check when buying anything from a chemist, whether on prescription or not. If you are not sure about a substance, check with the Sports Council Doping Control Unit, Walkden House, 3–10 Melton Street, London NW1 2EB. They have an enquiry hotline: 0171-383 2244.

Refusal to take a test

Refusing to take a test by the Sports Council Doping Control Unit Independent Sampling Officers (ISOs) is regarded as the same as if you had produced a positive test, but you will not have a 'B' sample for a second check.

And finally ...

The penalty that the British Judo Association gives to a player found to test positive depends on a number of factors. The fact that the player was tested positive in another sport makes no difference. The BJA policy is to carry whatever penalty was given in the other sport into the player's judo activities. The British Olympic Association (BOA) also has a rule for anyone found guilty of giving a positive test. He or she will *never* compete in the Olympic Games again.

10 CHAMPIONS

EUROPEAN CHAMPIONS – MEN

The Senior European Championships began in Paris as early as 1951. Those early years were very mixed as far as categories were concerned, so I have listed the European champions only from 1966.

1966   **Luxemburg**
Under 63kg:	Jean Claude Susline	(USSR)
Under 70kg:	Oleg Stepanov	(USSR)
Under 80kg:	Peter Snijders	(Netherlands)
Under 93kg:	Gouweleeuw	(Netherlands)
Over 93kg:	Wilhelm Ruska	(Netherlands)
Open:	Anzor Kiknadze	(USSR)

1967   **Milan**
Under 63kg:	Jean Claude Susline	(USSR)
Under 70kg:	Armand Desmet	(France)
Under 80kg:	Wladimir Pokataev	(USSR)
Under 93kg:	Peter Hermann	(FRG)
Over 93kg:	Wilhelm Ruska	(Netherlands)
Open:	Anton Geesink	(Netherlands)

1968   **Lausanne**
Under 63kg:	Markoplitchvili	(USSR)
Under 70kg:	Magaltadze	(USSR)
Under 80kg:	Wolfgang Hoffmann	(FRG)
Under 93kg:	Peter Hermann	(FRG)
Over 93kg:	Klaus Glahn	(FRG)
Open:	Saunine	(USSR)

1969   **Ostend**
Under 63kg:	Serge Feist	(France)
Under 70kg:	David Rudman	(USSR)
Under 80kg:	Bondarenko	(USSR)
Under 93kg:	Peter Snijders	(Netherlands)
Over 93kg:	Wilhelm Ruska	(Netherlands)
Open:	Wilhelm Ruska	(Netherlands)

1970   **Berlin**
Under 63kg:	Jean Mournier	(France)
Under 70kg:	Rudolf Hendel	(GDR)
Under 80kg:	Brian Jacks	(UK)
Under 93kg:	Pokataev	(USSR)
Over 93kg:	Klaus Glahn	(FRG)
Open:	K. Hennig	(GDR)

1971   **Gothenburg**
Under 63kg:	Jean Mournier	(France)
Under 70kg:	Rudolf Hendel	(GDR)
Under 80kg:	Guy Auffray	(France)
Under 93kg:	Hans Howiller	(GDR)
Over 93kg:	Wilhelm Ruska	(Netherlands)
Open:	Viktor Kusnetsov	(USSR)

1972   **The Hague**
Under 63kg:	Jean Mournier	(France)
Under 70kg:	Dietmar Hoetger	(GDR)
Under 80kg:	Jean-Paul Coche	(France)
Under 93kg:	Angelo Parisi*	(UK)*
Over 93kg:	Wilhelm Ruska	(Netherlands)
Open:	Wilhelm Ruska	(Netherlands)

* Angelo Parisi married a Frenchwoman and changed his nationality to that of his bride. He was then excluded from international competition for four years. He returned, with devastating effect, in the 1977 European Championships.

1973   **Madrid**
Under 63kg:	Melnichenko	(USSR)
Under 70kg:	Dietmar Hoetger	(GDR)
Under 80kg:	Brian Jacks	(UK)
Under 93kg:	Jean-Luc Rouge	(France)
Over 93kg:	S. Ojeda	(Spain)
Open:	Sergei Novikov	(USSR)

1974   **London**
Under 63kg: Melnichenko   (USSR)
Under 70kg: Gunther Kruger   (GDR)
Under 80kg: Jean-Paul Coche   (France)
Under 93kg: Zuvela   (Yugoslavia)
Over 93kg: Givi Onaschvili   (USSR)
Open: Sergei Novikov   (USSR)

1975   **Lyons**
Under 63kg: Torsten Reissmann   (GDR)
Under 70kg: Vladimir Nevzerov   (USSR)
Under 80kg: Peter Reiter   (Poland)
Under 93kg: Dietmar Lorenz   (GDR)
Over 93kg: Nidzeradze   (USSR)
Open: Givi Onaschvili   (USSR)

1976   **Kiev**
Under 63kg: Josef Tuncsik   (Hungary)
Under 70kg: Valery Dvoinikov   (USSR)
Under 80kg: Jean-Paul Coche   (France)
Under 93kg: Tengiz
      Khouboulouri   (USSR)
Over 93kg: Sergei Novikov   (USSR)
Open: Kazatchenkov   (USSR)

1977   **Ludwigshafen**
Under 60kg: Pogorelov   (USSR)
Under 65kg: Yves Delvingt   (France)
Under 71kg: Vladimir Nevzerov   (USSR)
Under 78kg: Adamczyk   (Poland)
Under 86kg: Alexei Volossov   (USSR)
Under 95kg: Dietmar Lorenz   (GDR)
Over 95kg: Jean-Luc Rouge   (France)
Open: Angelo Parisi   (France)

1978   **Helsinki**
Under 60kg: Felice Mariani   (Italy)
Under 65kg: Torsten Reissmann   (GDR)
Under 71kg: Gunther Kruger   (GDR)
Under 78kg: Harold Heinke   (GDR)
Under 86kg: Alexander Laskevitch   (USSR)
Under 95kg: Dietmar Lorenz   (GDR)
Over 95kg: Adelaar   (Netherlands)
Open: Dietmar Lorenz   (GDR)

1979   **Brussels**
Under 60kg: Felice Mariani   (Italy)
Under 65kg: Nikolai Soloduchin   (USSR)
Under 71kg: Neil Adams   (UK)
Under 78kg: Harold Heinke   (GDR)

Under 86kg: Jurg Rothlisberger   (Switzerland)
Under 95kg: Tengiz
      Khouboulouri   (USSR)
Over 95kg: Jean-Luc Rouge   (France)
Open: Tiurin   (USSR)

1980   **Vienna**
Under 60kg: Felice Mariani   (Italy)
Under 65kg: Torsten Reissmann   (GDR)
Under 71kg: Vlad   (Romania)
Under 78kg: Neil Adams   (UK)
Under 86kg: Alexander Laskevitch   (USSR)
Under 95kg: Jean-Luc Rouge   (France)
Over 95kg: Tiurin   (USSR)
Open: Robert Van de Walle   (Belgium)

1981   **Debrecen**
Under 60kg: Dziemianiuk   (Poland)
Under 65kg: Constantine Nicolae   (Romania)
Under 71kg: Karl Lehmann   (GDR)
Under 78kg: Georgi Petrov   (Bul)
Under 86kg: David Bodavelli   (USSR)
Under 95kg: Roger Vachon   (France)
Over 95kg: Gregory Veritchev   (USSR)
Open: Wojciech Reszko   (Poland)

1982   **Rostock**
Under 60kg: Khazret Tletseri   (USSR)
Under 65kg: Torsten Reissmann   (GDR)
Under 71kg: Ezio Gamba   (Italy)
Under 78kg: Mircea Fratica   (Romania)
Under 86kg: Alexander
      Iaskevitch   (USSR)
Under 95kg: Peter Kostenberger   (Austria)
Over 95kg: Henry Stoehr   (GDR)
Open: Tiurin   (USSR)

1983   **Paris**
Under 60kg: Khazret Tletseri   (USSR)
Under 65kg: Thierry Rey   (France)
Under 71kg: Ricard Melillo   (France)
Under 78kg: Neil Adams   (UK)
Under 86kg: Vitaly Pesniak   (USSR)
Under 95kg: Valerie Divisenko   (USSR)
Over 95kg: Khabil Biktachev   (USSR)
Open: Angelo Parisi   (France)

1984   **Liege**
Under 60kg: Khazret Tletseri   (USSR)
Under 65kg: Marc Alexandre   (France)

Under 71kg:	Tamaz Namgalauri	(USSR)
Under 78kg:	Neil Adams	(UK)
Under 86kg:	Vitaly Pesniak	(USSR)
Under 95kg:	Gunther Neureuther	(FRG)
Over 95kg:	Alexander von der Groeben	(FRG)
Open:	Angelo Parisi	(UK)

1985 **Hamar**

Under 60kg:	Khazret Tletseri	(USSR)
Under 65kg:	Ilieu Serban	(Romania)
Under 71kg:	Tamaz Namgalauri	(USSR)
Under 78kg:	Neil Adams	(UK)
Under 86kg:	Vitaly Pesniak	(USSR)
Under 95kg:	Robert Van de Walle	(Belgium)
Over 95kg:	Grigory Veritchev	(USSR)
Open:	Alexander von der Groeben	(FRG)

1986 **Belgrade**

Under 60kg:	Josef Czak	(Hungary)
Under 65kg:	Yuri Sokolov	(USSR)
Under 71kg:	Bertalan Hajtos	(Hungary)
Under 78kg:	Frank Wieneke	(FRG)
Under 86kg:	Peter Seisenbacher	(Austria)
Under 95kg:	Robert Van de Walle	(Belgium)
Over 95kg:	Willy Wilhelm	(Netherlands)
Open:	Henry Stoehr	(GDR)

1987 **Paris**

Under 60kg:	Patrick Roux	(France)
Under 65kg:	Jean-Pierre Hansen	(France)
Under 71kg:	Wieslaw Blach	(Poland)
Under 78kg:	Bashir Varaev	(USSR)
Under 86kg:	Fabien Canu	(France)
Under 95kg:	Koba Kurtanidze	(USSR)
Over 95kg:	Mihail Cioc	(Romania)
Open:	Grigory Veritchev	(USSR)

1988 **Pamplona**

Under 60kg:	Amiran Totikachvili	(USSR)
Under 65kg:	Bruno Carabetta	(France)
Under 71kg:	Joaquin Ruiz	(Spain)
Under 78kg:	Bashir Varaev	(USSR)
Under 86kg:	Fabien Canu	(France)
Under 95kg:	Jiri Sosna	(Czechoslovakia)

Over 95kg:	Grigory Veritchev	(USSR)
Open:	Elvis Gordon	(UK)

1989 **Helsinki**

Under 60kg:	Amiran Totikachvili	(USSR)
Under 65kg:	Bruno Carabetta	(France)
Under 71kg:	Jorma Korhonen	(Finland)
Under 78kg:	Bashir Varaev	(USSR)
Under 86kg:	Fabien Canu	(France)
Under 95kg:	Koba Kurtanidze	(USSR)
Over 95kg:	Rafael Kubacki	(Poland)
Open:	Juha Salonen	(Finland)

1990 **Frankfurt**

Under 60kg:	Philippe Padayrol	(France)
Under 65kg:	Bruno Carabetta	(France)
Under 71kg:	Guido Schumacher	(FRG)
Under 78kg:	Bashir Varaev	(USSR)
Under 86kg:	Waldemar Legien	(Poland)
Under 95kg:	Stephane Traineau	(France)
Over 95kg:	Sergei Kosorotov	(USSR)
Open:	Ramlo Tolnai	(Hungary)

1991 **Prague**

Under 60kg:	Philippe Pradayrol	(France)
Under 65kg:	Eric Born	(Switzerland)
Under 71kg:	Stephan Dott	(FRG)
Under 78kg:	Anton Wurth	(Netherlands)
Under 86kg:	Axel Lobenstein	(FRG)
Under 95kg:	Theo Maijerrs	(Netherlands)
Over 95kg:	Henery Stoehr	(FRG)
Open:	Igor Bereznitski	(USSR)

1992 **Paris**

Under 60kg:	Nazim Gousseinov	(Combined team from Soviet countries)
Under 65kg:	Benoit Campargue	(France)
Under 71kg:	Norbert Haimberger	(Austria)
Under 78kg:	Marko Spittka	(Germany)
Under 86kg:	Pascal Tayot	(France)
Under 95kg:	Stephane Traineau	(France)
Over 95kg:	Frank Moller	(Germany)
Open:	Tomas Muller	(Germany)

1993 **Athens**

Under 60kg:	Nazim Gousseinov	(Azerbaijan)
Under 65kg:	Sergei Kosmynin	(Russia)

Under 71kg:	Vladimir Dgebouadze	(Georgia)
Under 78kg:	Darcel Yandzi	(France)
Under 86kg:	Pascal Tayot	(France)
Under 95kg:	Stephane Traineau	(France)
Over 95kg:	David Khakhaleichvili	(Georgia)
Open:	David Khakhaleichvili	(Georgia)

1994   **Gdansk**

Under 60kg:	Girolamo Giovinazzo	(Italy)
Under 65kg:	Viktor Drachko	(Russia)
Under 71kg:	Sergei Kosmynin	(Russia)
Under 78kg:	Ryan Birch	(UK)
Under 86kg:	Oleg Maltsev	(Russia)
Under 95kg:	Pawel Nastula	(Poland)
Over 95kg:	David Douillet	(France)
Open:	Laurent Crost	(France)

1995   **Birmingham**

Under 60kg:	Nigel Donohue	(UK)
Under 65kg:	Peter Schlatter	(Germany)
Under 71kg:	Martin Schmidt	(Germany)
Under 78kg:	Patrick Reiter	(Austria)
Under 86kg:	Maartens Arens	(Netherlands)
Under 95kg:	Pawel Nastula	(Poland)
Over 95kg:	Sergei Kossorotov	(Russia)
Open:	Imre Csosz	(Hungary)

EUROPEAN CHAMPIONS – WOMEN

Like the World Championships, women fought at a completely separate venue and date from the men. This continued until 1987 in Paris when the Men's and Women's European Championships were combined. The 1988 Championships in Pamplona also introduced another innovation – the coloured judogi.

1975   **Munich**

Under 48kg:	Edith Hrovat	(Austria)
Under 52kg:	Christine Herzog	(France)
Under 56kg:	Sigrid Happ	(FRG)
Under 61kg:	Martine Rottier	(France)
Under 66kg:	Paulette Fouillet	(France)
Under 72kg:	Catherine Pierre	(France)
Over 72kg:	Chris Child	(UK)
Open:	Catherine Pierre	(France)

1976   **Vienna**

Under 48kg:	Jane Bridge	(UK)
Under 52kg:	Edith Hrovat	(Austria)
Under 56kg:	Sigrid Happ	(FRG)
Under 61kg:	Marine Rottier	(France)
Under 66kg:	Paulette Fouillet	(France)
Under 72kg:	Catherine Pierre	(France)
Over 72kg:	Christianne Kieburg	(FRG)
Open:	Laura di Toma	(Italy)

1977   **Arlon**

Under 48kg:	A. Hillesheim	(FRG)
Under 52kg:	Edith Hrovat	(Austria)
Under 56kg:	Sigrid Happ	(FRG)
Under 61kg:	Ingrid Berg	(FRG)
Under 66kg:	Czerwinsky	(FRG)
Under 72kg:	Catherine Pierre	(France)
Over 72kg:	Christianne Kieburg	(FRG)
Open:	Jocelyne Triadou	(France)

1978   **Cologne**

Under 48kg:	Jane Bridge	(UK)
Under 52kg:	Edith Hrovat	(Austria)
Under 56kg:	Gerda Winklebauer	(Austria)
Under 61kg:	Ingrid Berg	(FRG)
Under 66kg:	Katherine Krueger	(FRG)
Under 72kg:	Barbara Classen	(FRG)
Over 72kg:	Christianne Kieburg	(FRG)
Open:	Rothacher	(Switzerland)

1979   **Kerkrade**

Under 48kg:	Edith Bouthemy	(France)
Under 52kg:	Edith Hrovat	(Austria)
Under 56kg:	Gerda Winklebauer	(Austria)
Under 61kg:	Brigitte Deydier	(France)
Under 66kg:	Marie Mill	(Belgium)
Under 72kg:	Jocelyne Triadou	(France)
Over 72kg:	Christianne Kieburg	(FRG)
Open:	Barbara Classen	(FRG)

1980   **Udine**

Under 48kg:	Jane Bridge	(UK)
Under 52kg:	Montaguti	(Italy)
Under 56kg:	Gerda Winklebauer	(Austria)
Under 61kg:	Laura di Toma	(Italy)
Under 66kg:	Catherine Pierre	(France)
Under 72kg:	Jocelyne Triadou	(France)
Over 72kg:	Marguerite de Cal	(Italy)
Open:	Barbara Classen	(FRG)

1981 **Madrid**
Under 48kg:	Brigit Friedrich	(FRG)
Under 52kg:	Edith Hrovat	(Austria)
Under 56kg:	Gerda Winklebauer	(Austria)
Under 61kg:	Ann Hughes	(UK)
Under 66kg:	Marie Mill	(Belgium)
Under 72kg:	Jocelyne Triadou	(France)
Over 72kg:	Marguerite de Cal	(Italy)
Open:	Barbara Classen	(FRG)

1982 **Oslo**
Under 48kg:	Karen Briggs	(UK)
Under 52kg:	Edith Hrovat	(Austria)
Under 56kg:	Beatrice Rodriguez	(France)
Under 61kg:	Herta Reiter	(Austria)
Under 66kg:	Edith Simon	(Austria)
Under 72kg:	Jocelyne Triadou	(France)
Over 72kg:	Marjolene van Unen	(Netherlands)
Open:	Edith Simon	(Austria)

1983 **Genoa**
Under 48kg:	Karen Briggs	(UK)
Under 52kg:	Loretta Doyle	(UK)
Under 56kg:	Gerda Winklebauer	(Austria)
Under 61kg:	Ann Hughes	(UK)
Under 66kg:	Laura di Toma	(Italy)
Under 72kg:	Ingrid Berghmans	(Belgium)
Over 72kg:	Maria Motta	(Italy)
Open:	Ingrid Berghmans	(Belgium)

1984 **Pirmasens**
Under 48kg:	Karen Briggs	(UK)
Under 52kg:	Edith Hrovat	(Austria)
Under 56kg:	Diane Bell	(UK)
Under 61kg:	Martine Rottier	(France)
Under 66kg:	Brigitte Deydier	(France)
Under 72kg:	Barbara Classen	(FRG)
Over 72kg:	Marjolene van Unen	(Netherlands)
Open:	Natalina Lupino	(France)

1985 **Landskrona**
Under 48kg:	Marie Colignon	(France)
Under 52kg:	Pascale Doger	(France)
Under 56kg:	Beatrice Rodriguez	(France)
Under 61kg:	Boguslawa Olechnowicz	(Poland)
Under 66kg:	Brigitte Deydier	(France)
Under 72kg:	Ingrid Berghmans	(Belgium)
Over 72kg:	Sandra Bradshaw	(UK)
Open:	Marjolene van Unen	(Netherlands)

1986 **London**
Under 48kg:	Karen Briggs	(UK)
Under 52kg:	Dominique Brun	(France)
Under 56kg:	Beatrice Rodriguez	(France)
Under 61kg:	Diane Bell	(UK)
Under 66kg:	Brigitte Deydier	(France)
Under 72kg:	Irene de Kok	(Netherlands)
Over 72kg:	Beata Maksymow	(Poland)
Open:	Irene de Kok	(Netherlands)

1987 **Paris**
Under 48kg:	Karen Briggs	(UK)
Under 52kg:	Dominique Brun	(France)
Under 56kg:	Catherine Arnaud	(France)
Under 61kg:	Boguslawa Olechnowicz	(Poland)
Under 66kg:	Chantal Han	(Netherlands)
Under 72kg:	Irene de Kok	(Netherlands)
Over 72kg:	Isabelle Pague	(France)
Open:	Ingrid Berghmans	(Belgium)

1988 **Pamplona**
Under 48kg:	Jessica Gal	(Netherlands)
Under 52kg:	Alessandra Giungi	(Italy)
Under 56kg:	Catherine Arnaud	(France)
Under 61kg:	Diane Bell	(UK)
Under 66kg:	Alexandra Schreiber	(FRG)
Under 72kg:	Ingrid Berghmans	(Belgium)
Over 72kg:	Angélique Seriese	(Netherlands)
Open:	Ingrid Berghmans	(Belgium)

1989 **Helsinki**
Under 48kg:	Cécile Nowak	(France)
Under 52kg:	Jaana Ronkainen	(Finland)
Under 56kg:	Catherine Arnaud	(France)
Under 61kg:	Catherine Fleury	(France)
Under 66kg:	Emanuella Pierantozzi	(Italy)
Under 72kg:	Ingrid Berghmans	(Belgium)
Over 72kg:	Angélique Seriese	(Netherlands)
Open:	Angélique Seriese	(Netherlands)

1990 **Frankfurt**
Under 48kg:	Cécile Nowak	(France)
Under 52kg:	Sharon Rendle	(UK)
Under 56kg:	Catherine Arnaud	(France)
Under 61kg:	Begona Gomez	(Spain)
Under 66kg:	Alexandra Schreiber	(FRG)
Under 72kg:	Karin Krueger	(FRG)
Over 72kg:	Christine Cicot	(France)
Open:	Sharon Lee	(UK)

1991 **Prague**

Under 48kg:	Cécile Nowak	(France)
Under 52kg:	Jessica Gal	(Netherlands)
Under 56kg:	Miriam Blasco	(Spain)
Under 61kg:	Susanne Nagy	(Hungary)
Under 66kg:	Isabelle Beauruelle	(France)
Under 72kg:	Laetitia Meignan	(France)
Over 72kg:	Beata Maksymow	(Poland)
Open:	Monique van de Lee	(Netherlands)

1992 **Paris**

Under 48kg:	Cécile Nowak	(France)
Under 52kg:	Loretta Cusack	(UK)
Under 56kg:	Nicola Fairbrother	(UK)
Under 61kg:	Boguslawa Olechnowicz	(Poland)
Under 66kg:	Emanuella Pierantozzi	(Italy)
Under 72kg:	Laetitia Meignan	(France)
Over 72kg:	Svetlana Gudarenko	(Combined team from Soviet countries)
Open:	Angélique Seriese	(Netherlands)

1993 **Athens**

Under 48kg:	Jana Perlberg	(Germany)
Under 52kg:	Almudena Munoz	(Spain)
Under 56kg:	Nicola Fairbrother	(UK)
Under 61kg:	Yael Arad	(Israel)
Under 66kg:	Alice Dubois	(France)
Under 72kg:	Laetitia Meignan	(France)
Over 72kg:	Monique van de Lee	(Netherlands)
Open:	Angélique Seriese	(Netherlands)

1994 **Gdansk**

Under 48kg:	Yolander Soler	(Spain)
Under 52kg:	Edith Krause	(Poland)
Under 56kg:	Jessica Gal	(Netherlands)
Under 61kg:	G. van de Cavaye	(Belgium)
Under 66kg:	Rowena Sweatman	(UK)
Under 72kg:	Ulla Werbrouck	(Belgium)
Over 72kg:	Angélique Seriese	(Netherlands)
Open:	Monique van de Lee	(Netherlands)

1995 **Birmingham**

Under 48kg:	Yolander Soler	(Spain)

Under 52kg:	Alessandra Giungi	(Italy)
Under 56kg:	Nicola Fairbrother	(UK)
Under 61kg:	Jenny Gal	(Netherlands)
Under 66kg:	Alice Dubois	(France)
Under 72kg:	Ulla Werbrouck	(Belgium)
Over 72kg:	S.Goundarenko	(Russia)
Open:	Angélique Seriese	(Netherlands)

WORLD CHAMPIONS – MEN

The first three World Championships were an Open weight only and therefore there was only one winner. In 1965 this was changed to three weight categories (light-weight, middleweight and heavyweight) plus an Open weight. The next Championship was held in 1967 when the categories had increased to five weights plus the Open. It stayed like this until the 1979 event, held in Paris, when the weights increased to the seven categories we know today, plus the Open weight.

1956 **Tokyo**

	Shokichi Natsui	(Japan)

1958 **Tokyo**

	Koji Sone	(Japan)

1961 **Paris**

	Anton Geesink	(Netherlands)

1965 **Rio de Janeiro**

Lightweight:	Hirofumi Matsuda	(Japan)
Middleweight:	Isao Okano	(Japan)
Heavyweight:	Anton Geesink	(Netherlands)
Open weight:	Isao Inokuma	(Japan)

1967 **Salt Lake City**

Under 63kg:	Takafumi Shigeoka	(Japan)
Under 70kg:	Hiroshi Minatoya	(Japan)
Under 80kg:	Eiji Maruki	(Japan)
Under 93kg:	Nobayuki Sato	(Japan)
Over 93kg:	Wilhem Ruska	(Netherlands)
Open:	Mitsuo Matsunaga	(Japan)

1969   **Mexico City**
Under 63kg:	Yoshio Sonada	(Japan)
Under 70kg:	Horoshi Minatoya	(Japan)
Under 80kg:	Isamu Sonoda	(Japan)
Under 93kg:	Fumio Sasahara	(Japan)
Over 93k:	Shuji Suma	(Japan)
Open:	Masatoshi Shinomaki	(Japan)

1971   **Ludwigshafen**
Under 63k:	Takan Kawaguchi	(Japan)
Under 70k:	Hisashi Tsuzawa	(Japan)
Under 80k:	Shozo Fujii	(Japan)
Under 93kg:	Fumio Sasahara	(Japan)
Over 93kg:	Wilhelm Ruska	(Netherlands)
Open:	Masatoshi Shinomaki	(Japan)

1973   **Lausanne**
Under 63kg:	Yoshiharu Minami	(Japan)
Under 70kg:	Toyokazu Nomura	(Japan)
Under 80kg:	Shozo Fujii	(Japan)
Under 93kg:	Nobuyuki Sato	(Japan)
Over 93kg:	Chonosuke Takagi	(Japan)
Open:	Kasuhiro Ninomiya	(Japan)

1975   **Vienna**
Under 63kg:	Yoshiharu Minami	(Japan)
Under 70kg:	Vladimir Nevzerov	(USSR)
Under 80kg:	Shozo Fujii	(Japan)
Under 93kg:	Jean-Luc Rouge	(France)
Over 93kg:	Sumio Endo	(Japan)
Open:	Haruki Uemura	(Japan)

1979   **Paris**
Under 60kg:	Thierry Rey	(France)
Under 65kg:	Nicolai Soloduchin	(USSR)
Under 71kg:	Kyoito Katsuki	(Japan)
Under 78kg:	Shozo Fujii	(Japan)
Under 86kg:	Detlef Ultsch	(GDR)
Under 95kg:	Tengiz Khouboulouri	(USSR)
Over 95kg:	Yasuhiro Yamashita	(Japan)
Open:	Sumio Endo	(Japan)

1981   **Maastricht**
Under 60kg:	Yasuhiko Moriwake	(Japan)
Under 65kg:	Katsuihiko Kashiwazaki	(Japan)
Under 71kg:	Park Chong Ha	(Korea)
Under 78kg:	Neil Adams	(UK)
Under 86kg:	Bernard Tchoullouyan	(France)

Under 95kg:	Tengiz Khouboulouri	(USSR)
Over 95kg:	Yasuhiro Yamashita	(Japan)
Open:	Yasuhiro Yamashita	(Japan)

1983   **Moscow**
Under 60kg:	Khazret Tletseri	(USSR)
Under 65kg:	Nicolai Soloduchin	(USSR)
Under 71kg:	Hidetoshi Nakanishi	(Japan)
Under 78kg:	Nobutoshi Hikage	(Japan)
Under 86kg:	Detlef Ultsch	(GDR)
Under 95kg:	Andreas Preschel	(GDR)
Over 95kg:	Yasuhiro Yamashita	(Japan)
Open:	Hitoshi Saito	(Japan)

1985   **Seoul**
Under 60kg:	Shinji Hosokawa	(Japan)
Under 65kg:	Yuri Sokolov	(USSR)
Under 71kg:	Byung Keun Ahn	(Korea)
Under 78kg:	Nobutoshi Hikage	(Japan)
Under 86kg:	Peter Seisenbacher	(Austria)
Under 95kg:	Hitoshi Sugai	(Japan)
Over 95kg:	Yong-Chul Cho	(Korea)
Open:	Yoshimi Masaki	(Japan)

1987   **Essen**
Under 60kg:	Jae Yup Kim	(Korea)
Under 65kg:	Yosuke Yamamoto	(Japan)
Under 71kg:	Michael Swain	(USA)
Under 78kg:	Hirotaka Okada	(Japan)
Under 86kg:	Fabien Canu	(France)
Under 95kg:	Hitoshi Sugai	(Japan)
Over 95kg:	Gregory Veritchev	(USSR)
Open:	Naoya Ogawa	(Japan)

1989   **Belgrade**
Under 60kg:	Amiran Totikachvili	(USSR)
Under 65kg:	Dragomir Becanovic	(Yugoslavia)
Under 71kg:	Toshihiko Koga	(Japan)
Under 78kg:	Byung Ju Kim	(Korea)
Under 86kg:	Fabien Canu	(France)
Under 95kg:	Koba Kurtanidze	(USSR)
Over 95kg:	Naoya Ogawa	(Japan)
Open:	Naoya Ogawa	(Japan)

1991   **Barcelona**
Under 60kg:	Tadanori Koshino	(Japan)
Under 65kg:	Udo Quelmalz	(Germany)
Under 71kg:	Toshihiko Koga	(Japan)
Under 78kg:	Daniel Lascau	(Germany)
Under 86kg:	Hirotaka Okada	(Japan)

Under 95kg:	Stephane Traineau	(France)
Over 95kg:	Sergei Kosorotov	(USSR)
Open:	Naoya Ogawa	(Japan)

1993 **Hamilton**

Under 60kg:	Ryuki Sonoda	(Japan)
Under 65kg:	Yukimasa Nakamura	(Japan)
Under 71kg:	Hoon Chung	(Korea)
Under 78kg:	Ki-Young Chun	(Korea)
Under 86kg:	Yoshio Nakamura	(Japan)
Under 95kg:	Antal Kovacs	(Hungary)
Over 95kg:	David Douillet	(France)
Open:	Rafael Kubacki	(Poland)

1995 **Makuhari**

Under 60kg:	N. Ojeguine	(Russia)
Under 65kg:	Udo Quellmaz	(Germany)
Under 71kg:	Daisuke Hideshima	(Japan)
Under 78kg:	Toshihiko Koga	(Japan)
Under 86kg:	Ki-Young Jeon	(Korea)
Under 95kg:	Pawel Nastula	(Poland)
Over 95kg:	David Douillet	(France)
Open:	David Douillet	(France)

WORLD CHAMPIONS – WOMEN

The Women's World Championships were first held during the 'rest' year for the men's event. In 1987 the men and women joined forces and nowadays the World Championships are a combined men/women event.

The weight categories had already been set for a number of years before the first event so they were always the normal seven weights, plus an Open weight.

1980 **New York**

Under 48kg:	Jane Bridge	(UK)
Under 52kg:	Edith Hrovat	(Austria)
Under 56kg:	Gerda Winklebauer	(Austria)
Under 61kg:	Anita Staps	(Netherlands)
Under 66kg:	Edith Simon	(Austria)
Under 72kg:	Jocelyne Triadou	(France)
Over 72kg:	Marguerite de Cal	(Italy)
Open:	Ingrid Berghmans	(Belgium)

1982 **Paris**

Under 48kg:	Karen Briggs	(UK)
Under 52kg:	Loretta Doyle	(UK)
Under 56kg:	Beatrice Rodriguez	(France)
Under 61kg:	Martine Rottier	(France)
Under 66kg:	Brigitte Deydier	(France)
Under 72kg:	Barbara Classen	(FRG)
Over 72kg:	Natalina Lupino	(France)
Open:	Ingrid Berghmans	(Belgium)

1984 **Vienna**

Under 48kg:	Karen Briggs	(UK)
Under 52kg:	Kaori Yamaguchi	(Japan)
Under 56kg:	Anne-Marie Burns	(USA)
Under 61kg:	Natasha Hernandez	(Venezuela)
Under 66kg:	Brigitte Deydier	(France)
Under 72kg:	Ingrid Berghmans	(Belgium)
Over 72kg:	Marie-Teresa Motta	(Italy)
Open:	Ingrid Berghmans	(Belgium)

1986 **Maastricht**

Under 48kg:	Karen Briggs	(UK)
Under 52kg:	Dominique Brun	(France)
Under 56kg:	Ann Hughes	(UK)
Under 61kg:	Diane Bell	(UK)
Under 66kg:	Brigitte Deydier	(France)
Under 72kg:	Irene de Kok	(Netherlands)
Over 72kg:	Fenglian Gao	(China)
Open:	Ingrid Berghmans	(Belgium)

1987 **Essen**

Under 48kg:	Zhongyun Li	(China)
Under 52kg:	Sharon Rendle	(UK)
Under 56kg:	Catherine Arnaud	(France)
Under 61kg:	Diane Bell	(UK)
Under 66kg:	Alexandra Schreiber	(FRG)
Under 72kg:	Irene de Kok	(Netherlands)
Over 72kg:	Fenglian Gao	(China)
Open:	Fenglian Gao	(China)

1989 **Belgrade**

Under 48kg:	Karen Briggs	(UK)
Under 52kg:	Sharon Rendle	(UK)
Under 56kg:	Catherine Arnaud	(France)
Under 61kg:	Catherine Fleury	(France)
Under 66kg:	Emanuella Pierantozzi	(Italy)
Under 72kg:	Ingrid Berghmans	(Belgium)
Over 72kg:	Fenglian Gao	(China)
Open:	Estella Rodriguez	(Cuba)

1991	Barcelona	
Under 48kg:	Cécile Nowak	(France)
Under 52kg:	Alessandra Giungi	(Italy)
Under 56kg:	Miriam Blasco	(Spain)
Under 61kg:	Frauke Eickoff	(Germany)
Under 66kg:	Emanuella Pierantozzi	(Italy)
Under 72kg:	Mi-Jeong Kim	(Korea)
Over 72kg:	Ji-Yoo Moon	(Korea)
Open:	Xiaoyan Zhuang	(China)

1993	Hamilton	
Under 48kg:	Ryoko Tamura	(Japan)
Under 52kg:	Rodriguez Verdecia	(Cuba)
Under 56kg:	Nicola Fairbrother	(UK)
Under 61kg:	Caven van de Caveye	(Belgium)
Under 66kg:	Min-Sun Cho	(Korea)
Under 72kg:	Chunhui Leng	(China)
Over 72kg:	Johanna Hagn	(Germany)
Open:	Beata Maksymow	(Poland)

1995	Makuhari	
Under 48kg:	Ryoko Tamura	(Japan)
Under 52kg:	Marie-Claire Restoux	(France)
Under 56kg:	Driulis Gonzalez	(Cuba)
Under 61kg:	Sung Sook Jung	(Korea)
Under 66kg:	Min Sun Cho	(Korea)
Under 72kg:	Castellano Luna	(Cuba)
Over 72kg:	Angélique Seriese	(Netherlands)
Open:	Monique van der Lee	(Netherlands)

OLYMPIC CHAMPIONS – MEN

The first time judo was in the Olympic Games was in 1964. Each participating country was allowed to enter four players. These four could be in any weight – providing they made the weight – they chose. In theory, a country could have had all four players in one weight. The first round was fought in pools with just the number one player in each pool going through to the quarter-finals. From then on it was a straight knockout.

The second time judo appeared in the Olympic Games was at Munich in 1972. Politics affected the 1980 Games in Moscow when the Japanese, Koreans, Americans and West Germans did not send a team. The weights had changed again, this time to the modern categories. The contest length was reduced to five minutes and the IOC decided to introduce a policy of seeding the top competitors. The elimination method was to be a straightforward knockout and repêchage. To get a chance of a fight for the bronze medal, a player had to lose to one of the two finalists – the finalists being the two players, one from each side of the knock-out, who had not lost a contest all day.

Most of the Communist countries did not attend the 1984 Los Angeles Games. Yugoslavia, Romania and China were notable exceptions. The only major change at the 1988 Seoul Olympics was the removal of the Open weight group. In 1992 (Barcelona) the repêchage system was changed yet again. It now followed the European form of compound repêchage, which allowed a player back in for a chance of a bronze if he lost to a semi-finalist.

1964	Tokyo	
Under 68kg:	Takahide Nakatani	(Japan)
Under 80kg:	Isao Okano	(Japan)
Over 80kg:	Isao Inokuma	(Japan)
Open:	Anton Geesink	(Netherlands)

1972	Munich	
Under 63kg:	Takao Kawaguchi*	(Japan)
Under 70kg:	Toyokazu Nomura	(Japan)
Under 80kg:	Shinobu Sekine	(Japan)
Under 93kg:	Shota Chochosvilli	(USSR)
Over 93kg:	Wilhelm Ruska	(Netherlands)
Open:	Wilhelm Ruska	(Netherlands)

* Kawaguchi's opponent (Buidaa of Mongolia) failed a drug test (the first positive test in judo competitive history) and had his medal taken away.

1976	**Montreal**	
Under 63kg:	Hector Rodriguez	(Cuba)
Under 70kg:	Vladimir Nevzerov	(USSR)
Under 80kg:	Isamu Sonoda	(Japan)
Under 93kg:	Kazuhiro Ninomiya	(Japan)
Over 93kg:	Sergei Novikov	(USSR)
Open:	Haruki Uemura	(Japan)

1980	**Moscow**	
Under 60kg:	Thiery Rey	(France)
Under 65kg:	Nikolai Soloduchin	(USSR)
Under 71kg:	Ezio Gamba	(Italy)
Under 78kg:	Shota Khabarelli	(USSR)
Under 86kg:	Jurge Rothlisberger	(Switzerland)
Under 95kg:	Robert Van de Walle	(Belgium)
Over 95kg:	Angelo Parisi**	(France)
Open:	Dietmar Lorenz	(GDR)

** Parisi had won a bronze medal fighting for the UK in Munich in 1972.

1984	**Los Angeles**	
Under 60kg:	Shinji Hosokawa	(Japan)
Under 65kg:	Yoshiyuki Matsuoka	(Japan)
Under 71kg:	Byun-Keun Ahn	(Korea)
Under 78kg:	Frank Wieneke	(FRG)
Under 86kg:	Peter Seisenbacher	(Austria)
Under 95kg:	Hyung-Zoo Ha	(Korea)
Over 95kg:	Hitoshi Saito	(Japan)
Open:	Yasuhiro Yamashita	(Japan)

1988	**Seoul**	
Under 60kg:	Jae-Yup Kim	(Korea)
Under 65kg:	Kyung Keun Lee	(Korea)
Under 71kg:	Marc Alexandre	(France)
Under 78kg:	Waldemar Legien	(Poland)
Under 86kg:	Peter Seisenbacher	(Austria)
Under 95kg:	Aurelio Miguel	(Brazil)
Over 95kg:	Hitoshi Saito	(Japan)

1992	**Barcelona**	
Under 60kg:	Nazim Gousseinov	(A combined team from Soviet countries, formed after the dis-solution of the USSR))
Under 65kg:	Rogerio Sampaio	(Brazil)

Under 71kg:	Toshihiko Koga	(Japan)
Under 78kg:	Hidehiko Yoshida	(Japan)
Under 86kg:	Waldemar Legien	(Poland)
Under 95kg:	Antal Kovacs	(Hungary)
Over 95kg:	David Khakhaleichvili	(Combined team from Soviet countries)

OLYMPIC CHAMPIONS – WOMEN

Women's judo first appeared at the Olympic Games in Seoul, Korea. Like all 'new' sports it was a 'demonstration sport'. Although the participants could not, officially, call themselves Olympic champions I have included the results.

1988	**Seoul**	
Under 48kg:	Zhongyun Li	(China)
Under 52kg:	Sharon Rendle	(UK)
Under 56kg:	Suzanne Williams	(Australia)
Under 61kg:	Diane Bell	(UK)
Under 66kg:	Hikari Sasaki	(Japan)
Under 72kg:	Ingrid Berghmans	(Belgium)
Over 72kg:	Angélique Seriese	(Netherlands)

1992	**Barcelona**	
Under 48kg:	Cécile Nowak	(France)
Under 52kg:	Almudena Munoz	(Spain)
Under 56kg:	Miriam Blasco	(Spain)
Under 61kg:	Catherine Fleury	(France)
Under 66kg:	Odalis Reve	(Cuba)
Under 72kg:	Mi-Jeong Kim	(Korea)
Over 72kg:	Xiaoyan Zhuang	(China)

For further information, there is an excellent book by Oon Oon Yeoh, a Korean judo expert, entitled *Great Judo Championships of the World,* published by Ippon Books, 1993, which lists every medal winner in World, Olympic and European Championships (both Senior and Junior). There are also a number of other important tournaments listed and some interesting historical details about each event.

11 JUDO TERMS, THEIR PRONUNCIATION AND TRANSLATION

I will begin with a reminder of the pronunciation. Generally, vowels are usually short and explosive sounds. The letter 'A' is pronounced as in hat (except at the start of a word, when it changes to something like the 'U' in hut); the 'E' as in get; the 'I' as in hit; the 'O' as in hot; and the 'U' as in hut (except where I have put a macron above the letter thus – *ū* It is then pronounced like the double 'O' in boot).

Japanese word	Pronunciation	Translation
arigato	*ari-ga-toh*	thank you
ashi	*ash-ee*	leg or foot
ate	*ah-teh*	hit or strike
atemiwaza	*ah-teh-me-wa-za*	punching technique
awasete	*ah-wah-seh-teh*	joined together
būshido	*boo-she-doh*	way of the warrior
chūi	*chew-i*	(*lit.* attention) a penalty equivalent to a *yuko* score to a player's opponent
Dan	*dan*	(*lit.* step) a black belt judo grade. They go from 1st Dan to, theoretically, 12th Dan; 10th Dan is the highest ever awarded. The highest judo Dan grade awarded in the UK is 9th Dan. You can be awarded a Dan grade in almost any pastime in Japan from chess to ikebana (flower arranging)
de	*day*	advance or advancing
do	*doh*	'the Way' as in judo – the Gentle Way
do	*doh*	the trunk of the body. A typical example of a Japanese word having more than one different meaning
dojo	*doh-joh*	(*lit.* the Hall of the Way) a place where judo and other martial arts are practised
domo arigato	*doh-moh-ari-gah-toh*	thank you very much
eri	*eh-ri*	neckband or collar of the jacket
fūsen gachi	*foo-zen-ga-chi*	win by non-appearance of a player's opponent
gaeshi	*ga-eh-shi*	to counter; sometimes spelt as *kaeshi*
gake	*ga-kay*	hook or block

Japanese word	Pronunciation	Translation
garami	*ga-rah-mi*	entangle or wrap
gatame	*ga-tah-may*	(*lit.* to harden) in judo it means to hold
go	*goh*	five, fifth
go	*goh*	an ancient Japanese territorial board game
go-no-sen-no-kata	*goh-noh-sen-noh-ka-ta*	forms of counter techniques
goshin jitsū	*goh-shin-jit-soo*	self-defence
goshi	*goh-shi*	hip; also spelt *koshi*
gurūma	*guh-roo-mah*	wheel; also spelt *kuruma*
gyaku	*gee-ya-kuh*	reverse
hachi	*ha-chi*	eight, eighth
hadaka	*ha-da-ka*	bare or naked
hajime	*ha-ji-may*	begin
hajimemashite	*ha-ji-may-mash-teh*	Good morning. Greeting used up to around 10 a.m. See also *konnichiwa* and *kombanwa*
hane	*ha-neh*	spring or jump
hansoku	*han-soh-kuh*	Disqualification. A penalty equivalent to giving a player's opponent an *ippon* win.
hantei	*han-teh-i*	Judgement or decision asked for by the referee when the scores are equal at the end of a contest. The judges and referee simultaneously raise a red or white flag according to whom they consider has won
hara	*ha-ra*	abdomen or belly
harai	*ha-ra-i*	sweep; sometimes spelt *barai*
hidari	*hi-da-ri*	left as opposed to right
hiki	*hi-ki*	pull; sometimes spelt *hikki*
hiza	*hi-za*	knee
hon	*hon*	basic
ichi	*i-chi*	one, first
ippon	*i-pon*	one point. The ultimate score in judo
itsūtsū-no-kata	*it-soot-soo-noh-ka-ta*	forms of five. A series of techniques demonstrated together in a very formalized manner
jigotai	*jih-goh-tah-i*	defensive attitude/posture
joseki	*joh-seh-ki*	place of honour in the *dojo* where guests or the most senior players sit during a training session. A player should always bow to *joseki* when stepping on to a mat as a mark of respect. If there is no physical *joseki* it is usually accepted as being directly opposite a player as he steps on the mat
jū	*joo*	ten, tenth

Japanese word	Pronunciation	Translation
jū	*joo*	gentle, as in judo 'the Gentle Way'. It is a difficult concept to explain to a Westerner. Gentle in this instance means giving as a willow tree gives and bends to the force of a strong wind. By so doing, the wind goes where the tree wants – around it rather than blowing it over
jū	*joo*	gun
jūdo	*joo-doh*	the Way of Gentleness (see above)
jūdogi	*joo-doh-gi*	Clothing worn to practise judo. Comprises a jacket, trousers and a belt. Sometimes abbreviated to *gi*
jūdoka	*joo-doh-ka*	someone who practises judo
jūjitsū	*joo-jit-soo*	Japanese self-defence art, the forerunner of judo. It is an art that is still practised
jūno kata	*joo-noh-ka-ta*	forms of gentleness. A demonstration of techniques which highlight 'giving way'
kaeshiwaza	*ka-eh-shi-wa-za*	counter-techniques. See also *gaeshi*
kai or *kwai*	*k-eye*	society or club (in *kwai* the letter 'W' is silent)
kake	*ka-keh*	the point where a throw takes effect
kami	*ka-mi*	hair
kami	*ka-mi*	paper
kami	*ka-mi*	upper
kansetsūwaza	*kan-set-soo-wa-za*	locking techniques. Applies to all joints, but only those against the elbow joint are allowed in judo
kao	*ka-oh*	face
kata	*ka-ta*	form. A very formalized demonstration of a set of judo techniques
kata	*ka-ta*	shoulder
katsū	*kat-soo*	resuscitation. Usually used to bring round players unconscious from a strangle. Uses points on the body, rather like acupuncture, but without the needles
keiko	*keh-i-koh*	training, practice
keikoku	*keh-i-koh-koo*	warning. A penalty which gives the opponent a *waza-ari* score in a judo contest
kesa	*keh-sah*	a monk's sash which is worn diagonally across his chest
kiai	*ki-ah-i*	a shout used to help exert maximum effort; the shout is meant to come from the stomach
kikengachi	*ki-ken-gah-chi*	win due to opponent withdrawing during contest because of injury
kimenokata	*ki-meh-noh-ka-ta*	forms of decision or actual fighting
ko	*koh*	ancient

Japanese word	Pronunciation	Translation
ko	*koh*	arc
ko	*koh*	minor
Kodokan	*koh-doh-kan*	the spiritual home of judo. The headquarters of judo in Tokyo, Japan
koka	*koh-ka*	(*lit.* effect) the lowest score which appears on a scoreboard. Usually described as 'almost *yuko*'
kombanwa	*kom-ban-wah*	good evening. Greeting used after dusk
konnichiwa	*koh-ni-chi-wah*	hello. Used after 10 a.m. until dusk. See also *hajimemashite* and *kombanwa*
koshiwaza	*koh-shi-wah-zah*	hip techniques
koshikinokata	*koh-shi-ki-noh-ka-ta*	forms ancient. A formalized demonstration of old judo techniques
kūbi	*koo-bi*	neck
kumikata	*kuh-mi-ka-ta*	gripping, taking hold
kuzure	*kuh-zuh-reh*	to break or broken
kuzushi	*kuh-zuh-shi*	to disturb the balance of a player
kyū	*ki-yoo*	nine, ninth
kyū	*ki-yoo*	pupil grade in judo. The *judoka* who wear coloured belts
ma	*mah*	exactly
makikomi	*mah-ki-koh-mi*	(*lit.* to wrap up) commonly known as 'winding throw'. This is applied to a type of technique where a player pulls his opponent's arm round him in order to trap him as he rolls into the throw
masūtemiwaza	*mah-soo-teh-mi-wa-za*	rear sacrifice technique
mata	*mah-tah*	upper/inner thigh
matte	*mat-teh*	wait. Referee's instruction. Temporarily halts the contest and brings both players back to the centre of the contest area
migi	*mi-gi*	right as opposed to left
Mon	*mon*	(*lit.* gate) in British judo it is applied to junior *judoka* grades. The belt colours are the same as the senior Kyu grades but there are three grades per colour. These are indicated by red stripes at the end of the belt
morote	*moh-roh-teh*	two hands
mune	*muh-neh*	chest
nage	*nah-geh*	throw
nagenokata	*nah-geh-noh-ka-ta*	form of throws. A very formalized demonstration of classical judo throws
nami	*nah-mi*	normal
nami	*nah-mi*	in line

Japanese word	Pronunciation	Translation
nana	*nah-nah*	seven, seventh; sometimes the word *shichi* is used
newaza	*neh-wa-za*	(*lit.* lying down techniques) ground techniques
ni	*nee*	two, second
o	*oh*	major
obi	*oh-bi*	belt or sash
okūri	*oh-koo-ri*	sliding
osaekomiwaza	*oh-sah-eh-koh-mi-wa-za*	holding technique. The referee calls '*Osaekomi*' to indicate to the timekeeper that the hold is on
otoshi	*oh-tosh-i*	drop
randori	*ran-doh-ri*	free-moving practice
rei	*reh-i*	bow
renrakuwaza	*ren-rah-kuh-wa-za*	combination technique
renshū	*ren-shoo*	practice
renzokūwaza	*ren-zoh-koo-wa-za*	linking or linked technique
roku	*roh-kuh*	six, sixth
ryū	*ree-oo*	school
ryū	*ree-oo*	dragon
samurai	*sah-muh-rye*	ancient Japanese warrior
san	*san*	three, third
sasai	*sah-sigh*	propping
sayōnara	*sah-yoh-na-ra*	goodbye. Used informally among friends
sensei	*sen-seh-i*	teacher
seoi	*seh-oh-i*	carry on the back
seoinage	*seh-oh-i-nah-geh*	normally translated as shoulder throw but, this is not quite correct
seppūkū	*sep-poo-koo*	the proper word for the ritual suicide usually, wrongly, referred to as *harakiri*
shi	*she*	four, fourth; sometimes the word *yon* is used
shiai	*shi-aye*	contest
shiaijo	*shi-aye-joh*	contest area
shichi	*shi-chi*	seven, seventh; sometimes the word *nana* is used
shido	*shi-doh*	(*lit.* guidance) penalty equivalent to a *koka* score for a player's opponent
shihan	*shi-han*	founder
shiho	*shi-hoh*	four quarters
shime	*shi-meh*	tighten
shime	*shi-meh*	strangle
shita	*sh-ta*	underneath
shizentai	*shi-zen-tie*	natural standing posture

Japanese word	Pronunciation	Translation
sode	*soh-day*	sleeve
sogogachi	*soh-goh-gah-chi*	a win in a contest where one player is penalized by *keikoku* and his opponent then scores a *waza-ari*. Equivalent to *waza-ari-awasete-ippon*
sonomama	*soh-noh-mah-mah*	(*lit.* as it is) referee's word to freeze the actions of the players during a contest
soremade	*soh-reh-mah-deh*	(*lit.* that is all) referee's word to end a contest
soto	*soh-toh*	outer or outside
sūkūi	*soo-koo-i*	scooping
sūmi	*soo-mi*	corner or angle
sūtemiwaza	*soo-teh-mi-wa-za*	(*lit.* throwaway technique) normally translated as sacrifice technique. A player sacrifices his standing position (i.e. throws himself to the ground) in order to throw his opponent
tachiwaza	*ta-chi-wa-za*	standing techniques
tai	*tah-i or tie*	body
tani	*ta-ni*	valley
taniotoshi	*ta-ni-o-tosh-i*	valley drop (a sacrifice throw)
tatami	*ta-tam-i*	straw mats used as floor covering in Japanese houses. Also used as mats in *dojos*. Although the originals were made from rice straw, the word *tatami* now generally refers to any type of judo mat
tate	*ta-teh*	length
te	*teh*	hand
tewaza	*teh-wa-za*	hand technique
tekūbi	*teh-koo-bi*	wrist
toketa	*toh-keh-ta*	referee's call to indicate that a player has escaped from a hold-down (*osaekomi*)
tokūiwaza	*toh-koo-i-wa-za*	favourite technique
tomoenage	*toh-moh-eh-na-geh*	(*lit.* turning-over throw) usually translated as stomach throw
tori	*toh-ri*	(*lit.* the taker) the player who executes a technique
tsūgiashi	*t-soo-gi-ash-i*	formalized walk used in *kata*. One foot leads, the other is then brought up to it but does not pass it. The first foot then takes another step
tsūkūri	*t-soo-koo-ri*	breaking your opponent's balance
tsūri	*t-soo-ri*	(*lit.* fishing) common translation is pulling, as in the next throw
tsūrikomiashi	*t-soo-ri-koh-mi-ash-i*	pulling propping ankle (throw)

Japanese word	Pronunciation	Translation
uchikomi	uh-chi-koh-mi	(lit. to beat against) a form of technique training where a player practises a throw to the point where it takes effect (kake) without actually throwing his partner
ude	uh-deh	arm
uke	uh-keh	(lit. receiver) the player who is thrown or on whom a technique is applied
ukemi	uh-keh-mi	breakfall
uki	uh-ki	float or floating
ura	uh-rah	reverse
ushiro	uh-shi-roh	back or behind
utsūri	ut-soo-ri	to change
wakare	wa-kah-reh	division or separation
waza	wa-za	technique
waza-ari	wa-za-a-ri	near technique. Usually translated as 'nearly ippon'
yama	ya-ma	mountain
yoko	yoh-koh	side
yon	yon	four, fourth; sometimes the word shi is used
yūbi	yoo-bi	finger
yūko	yoo-koh	(lit. effect) presumably a bigger effect than koka. Beats any number of kokas but can itself be beaten by waza-ari or ippon
yūseigachi	yoo-seh-i-gah-chi	win by superiority. The expression given when a win is as a result of the decision made at hantei by referee and judges
zarei	zah-reh-i	kneeling or sitting bow
zazen	zah-zen	meditation usually done in a sitting position
zero	zeh-roh	nought
zori	zoh-ri	sandals or slippers with a central strap gripped by the toes. Traditionally made with straw but the word is now applied to any similar slipper made from all sorts of material

It is better to remember the individual words rather than complete phrases. For example, *kuzure yokoshihogatame* can be split into four words: *kuzure* meaning broken, *yoko* meaning side, *shiho* meaning four quarters, *gatame* meaning hold down'.

By breaking the phrases down, as in the above example, even if you have never heard of a technique, you can get a good idea of what you are supposed to be doing. For example, something every good judoka should be capable of at the start of a session, particularly those with a permanently laid mat in their *dojo*, is *deharaitatami*.

INDEX

Page numbers in *italic* refer to the illustrations